The Unbroken Thread

A HISTORY OF QUILTMAKING
IN THE CATSKILLS

Steve Hoare

Introduction by Carter Houck
Photography by Drew Harty

BLACK · DOME

BLACK DOME PRESS
RR 1, Box 422
Hensonville, NY 12439
518-734-6357 fax 518-734-5802

Published by

Black Dome Press Corp.
RR1, Box 422
Hensonville, New York 12439
(518) 734-6357
fax (518)-734-5802

First Edition, 1996

Library of Congress Cataloging-in-Publication Data
Hoare, Steve. 1952-
      The unbroken thread: a history of quiltmaking in the
Catskills/Steve Hoare: photographs by Drew Harty; with an introduc-
tion by Carter Houck.—1st ed.
         p. cm.
      Includes bibliographical references.
      ISBN 1-883789-07-9 (pbk.)
      1. Quiltmaking—New York (State)—Catskill Mountains Region—
History. 2. Quiltmakers—New York (State)—Catskill Mountains
Region—History—20th century. I. Title.
TT835.H54   1996
746.46'09747'38—dc20   96-301
                                                             CIP

Design by Carol Clement, Artemisia, Inc.
Printed in the USA

FRONT COVER: "Old Rip," 28" x 34" wall-hanging,
hand-appliqued and hand-quilted by Betty Verhoeven and Virginia Hull, 1995.

For all the quilters,
living and dead,
here and elsewhere;

and for Eleanor Ruth,
December's child,
star of wonder, star of light.

"There are certain things that these women seem to have had in common: and that was to make beautiful things; to touch immortality by leaving something behind; not to waste anything in God's creation but put them into something beautiful; and a concern for others, a very strong sense of community." [Hilda Pleva, quilt-maker, Kingston, 1993]

Table of Contents

Preface

It is obvious that quilters are people who love fabric and color and design. It is only slightly less obvious that they love words and descriptions and stories and—yes—gossip. Quilters store fabric as far as possible from the prying eyes of family members who cannot imagine to what useful purpose so much colorful and often cast-off stuff can be put. In those same houses there are usually shelves full of books, papers, patterns and old magazines. Books that tell about quilters and their lives are among the best histories of American women. In this volume Steven Hoare, a lifelong resident of the Catskill Mountains, has compiled a wonderful history of the 20th-century women of a little-known region of America. In spite of the proximity to New York City and Albany, the Catskills have remained a dreamy and distant place where living is not easy and where energy and persistence are the prime ingredients of daily life. Quilters know that those same qualities are necessary to starting and completing a quilt.

Each county in the Catskill region has its own personality and, to a large degree, its own climate. The lilacs bloom in Kingston three to four weeks before those in Tannersville, 30 miles away and nearly 2,000 feet higher. "On the mountain" it is said that there are two seasons, winter and the Fourth of July—an old saw but sometimes applicable. What better climate and conditions can be found for quilting! In the winter there are days when leaving the house seems much less productive than staying in at the quilt frame. In the summer, when many people find it too hot to keep the needle running through the cloth, there is always a spot with a breeze in much of this region. Of course group quilting serves the same purpose that it has in many areas for many decades, an excuse to get out of one's house and meet with friends in a place where there is not a demanding social life in any other form.

The freshness of the author's approach to the areas and the lives so well described in this book comes from diligent research and first-person contact with the people and places he so obviously enjoys. Each woman comes alive in her own voice, complete with her own view of life as well as of quilting. This is not just a book for quilters, but one for anyone who loves to delve into other lives and to marvel at the variety and even the foibles of individual personalities.

This is a book that can be put down and picked up at any point—there is no particular beginning or end. The opening is wonderfully fresh, even to those dedicated quilters who have read it all and heard it all. This may be a direct result of the author being a non-quilter who had to search out what was pertinent and separate it from the truly banal stories that have been too often repeated. For a true novice or a complete non-quilter, the opening is just enough to explain why one would want to know more about people who go on in an age of jets and computers, pushing a needle through fabric in an attempt to create something of utility and beauty.

In many ways this is not just a book about quilters in the Catskill Mountains—a place remembered largely for Rip Van Winkle who once took a record-breaking nap in the area—it is about people, and women especially, who make up America. There are those who are over 90 and still plying needle and thread, those who ran away from city areas in the '60s to escape a mind-numbing political fray, and those who had always sewed for their families and needed to find the ultimate way to use up the scraps. No matter why or how they set their feet on this path toward the quilting frame, they have found friends, a creative outlet, and the sanity to survive in an ever more confusing world. In reading this book, it seems that there is a message (or several of them) about lives and aims and goals and just plain having fun.

Carter Houck

Acknowledgments

Foremost among the many to whom this book owes its existence are Betty Verhoeven and Virginia Hull, former co-presidents of the Catskill Mountain Quilters Hall of Fame. Together they forged gamely ahead through the labyrinth of grant applications, never showing signs of discouragement in the face of disappointment or setback. They brought this project forward in a selfless manner, with an even-handedness and sense of fairness which was a credit to the position they were entrusted with. The patient encouragement and unfaltering support they gave their author is most deeply appreciated.

Deborah Allen, our publisher, was indefatigable in her efforts to ensure throughout every phase of this project that the final result would be as good a book as could be done. Her patience with her deadline-impaired author was no less than remarkable, her guidance indispensable, her judgment sound. She gives her best efforts to each book she publishes, insisting on consistently high quality and investing many hundreds of hours of hard work. No author could ask for more.

I am very grateful to Carter Houck for not only taking time from her very busy schedule to meet with me and discuss quiltmaking, but also for capturing succinctly and precisely in her fine introduction the essence of what I have tried to accomplish in this book.

I am indebted to Carol O'Beirne and The Erpf Catskill Cultural Center's Folklife Program for granting permission to freely use material from the Erpf Center's 1986 publication, *Catskill Mountain Quilters Hall of Fame* by Janis Benincasa. My essays on those inductees into the Hall of Fame who died prior to the summer of 1993 would have been sadly incomplete without the Center's gracious cooperation.

Written records of quiltmaking and quiltmakers prior to the early 1970s are scarce. I am grateful to Joyce Tompkins and the United Methodist Women of the Ashland Community Church for providing me with the diary kept by the Ladies' Sewing Circle of Mitchell Hollow, and to Kathleen Rolfs and the Claryville Reformed Church Ladies Aid Society for likewise providing me with their Secretary's Report. Those two volumes carried a few words of women and their quilts across the deep gulf separating us from the otherwise silent past.

The author's research was assisted by willing and expert help from many quarters, none more valuable than the region's museums, all of which maintain extensive collections of antique quilts. The following gave freely of their time and knowledge, and I extend to them my utmost gratitude: Shelby Kriele, curator of the Greene County Historical Society's Bronck House Museum; Patricia Millen and Carolyn Bennett, former and present curators, respectively, of the Zadock Pratt Museum; Marge Smith, president, and Pat Burns, museum chairperson, of the Sullivan County Historical Society; Ellen McHale, director of the Schoharie County Historical Society's Old Stone Fort; Anne Doerge and Harold Zoch of the Middleburg Library's Best House; Patricia Millen (once again), staff member of Kingston's Senate House State Historical Site; and Linda Norris, past director of the Delaware County Historical Association. The historical legacy of the Catskill Mountains is in fine hands.

Most books are a labor of love, but significant costs are still involved. Financial assistance came from several organizations, public and private. This book is made possible with public funds from the Decentralization Program of the New York State Council on the Arts, administered in Greene County by the Greene County Council on the Arts, with grants awarded in two successive years, 1993 and 1994; by public funds from the Decentralization Program of the New York State Council on the Arts, administered in Delaware County by The Roxbury Arts Group, with a grant awarded in 1993; by a timely and generous grant from The A. Lindsay and Olive B. O'Connor Foundation, Inc., awarded in 1994; and by donations from four member guilds of the Catskill Mountain Quilters Hall of Fame–Wiltwyck, the Schoharie Valley Piecemakers, the Calico Geese, and the Patchworkers. On behalf of myself and the Catskill Mountain Quilters Hall of Fame, I wish to thank the officers and members of all of the above organizations for their faith in the worthiness of this book and the women whose art it celebrates.

Special mention and thanks to two women who work very hard for their county's arts programs—Kay Stamer and Nancy Harding.

To Matina Billias, Jim Planck and Patricia H. Davis, who helped proofread the manuscript: thank you for your diligent search for errata.

And to my wife, Sarah Burrows, who encouraged me to undertake this project and who withstood the many many hours of neglect as I roamed the Catskills and sequestered myself to write: Thanks! It's finally over!

Steve Hoare

"Scrapaholic Nine-Patch" by Viola Scranton. Hand-appliqued and hand-quilted by Viola between May and August, 1991, when she was 81. Nine 9-inch squares, each of different fabric, were stacked, cut at random, and then assembled into "Nine-Patch" squares so that each fabric would be placed in a different position in each square.

CHAPTER 1

The Catskills

The five counties that comprise the Catskill Mountains region—Greene, Delaware, Sullivan, Schoharie and Ulster—do not fully share a common history, economy or ethnicity. IBM employees living in Kingston, the region's largest city (and New York State's first capital), may feel they have more in common with neighboring Hudson Valley dwellers in New Paltz or Poughkeepsie than with, say, dairy farmers in Delaware County or ski lift mechanics in Greene.

It is a huge geographic area, remarkably diverse within its stretching bounds. It borders Pennsylvania to the south, the Adirondacks to the north. To the east is the Hudson River; to the west are the vast fertile farmlands of New York, which even today make agriculture—not banking, manufacture, or retail—New York State's leading industry.

Tourism and recreation is New York's second most important economy, and it is this that now unites the Catskills. Whether they come to ski in Greene County, explore caves in Schoharie, attend a conference and play golf in Sullivan, hunt and fish in Delaware, or flock to a music festival in Ulster, the Catskills—if they are known at all—are known as one of America's playgrounds.

Not so for the local population, who call the Catskills "home." For them it is a daily economic struggle in an often inhospitable climate where winter is a six-month affair. The compensations are clean air, uncongested roads, a scattering of still-unshot wildlife, scenic beauty and great neighbors.

Henry Hudson saw the Catskills off in the blue distance as he sailed up the river that would soon thereafter bear his name. Following his explorations, Dutch settlements began to sprout up along the river and the tributary valleys but, even following the English appropriation of the colony, the mountains remained a natural barrier to further settlement. They were near, yet aloof and distant at the same time, forbidding and wild, unsettled even by Native American tribes, and thus fertile ground for lore and legend. They were part of America's first wilderness.

Much of that mountain wilderness did not begin to be tamed until after the Revolution, when land grants were awarded to veterans. A new migration from an already-crowded New England (especially Connecticut) added further impetus to westward expansion. Farms and sawmills began to dot the mountain hollows, roads and turnpikes were built, and by the turn of the nineteenth century most of the existing communities in the Catskills had had their start.

The first economy derived from the various fruits of the earth: in addition to the yield from farms, there was lumber for homes, bluestone for sidewalks, and hemlock trees for the tanning industry, to name but a few resources. But the construction of the turnpikes gave the region an important second economy, service-based, catering to the steady flow of immigrants ever westward and the return flow of farm and forest goods eastward to the Hudson.

For a few short decades, the river towns of the Catskills flourished with this trade until the Erie Canal diverted the flow of goods and passengers northward. They were saved from relegation to oblivion, however, by the almost simultaneous growth of the tourist and vacation industry in the Catskills, led by Greene County's Catskill Mountain House in the 1820s. The success and fame of the Mountain House led to growth and competition elsewhere in the region, and the Catskills became America's first destination resort.

The stream of visitors included many of the young republic's luminaries in the field of letters–Thoreau, Washington Irving, James Fenimore Cooper, and later, Mark Twain and William Cullen Bryant. Through their writings the Catskills entered into the young soul of the nation, and with the publication of *Rip Van Winkle,* the Catskills became a part of world literature.

Through Thoreau and Emerson, Boston and environs had become the birthplace of Transcendentalism. The Catskills, with its glens and glades, cascades and forest wilds, became the home and haunt of the Romantics. Thomas Cole led the way, and his followers became known as the Hudson River School of painters–America's first indigenous art movement. The legend of the "benign" wilderness was born.

By then, of course (the middle years of the nineteenth century), the Catskills were far from wild. The grand hotel era had been born, railroads crisscrossed the region, and steamboats plied the river. The Catskills had become "upstate," where wealthy and upper-middle-class metropolitan New Yorkers vacationed every summer. Gradually, the less affluent found a haven in the Catskills as well. The boarding house era was born as farmers opened their homes to lodgers who wanted an affordable taste of country life.

With the twentieth century, the rich and famous found other, more exotic, fashionable or exclusive playgrounds, but the Catskills continued to be a nearby haven for the less privileged. The grand hotels fell into decline while the middle-class family resorts prospered. Ethnicity played a role, and the Catskills became more diverse demographically as like sought to reside and consort with like. Italian, Irish and German communities developed, with resorts offering the tastes and cultures of the old countries. Sullivan County, perhaps the most dramatic example of this, became known as the "borscht belt" and "the Jewish Alps" for the large number of Jewish boarders–often excluded and ostracized elsewhere–who flocked to that county's hotels and bungalow communities for the summer months.

As the twentieth century draws to a close the Catskill Mountains remain largely a refuge or resource for the urbanite. The city casts its shadow, in every way, over the mountains. Family farms are disappearing–and with them, a way of life–and are being replaced by vacation homes. Scores of farms and some of the Catskills' most fertile bottom land now lie under man-made lakes built to quench the thirst of New York City, while watershed regulations make it increasingly harder for those few farms which have survived to continue to operate.

The creation of the Catskill State Park and Preserve is perhaps emblematic of the continuing trade-off as city and country try to coexist in a shrinking world. The "forever wild" status of the state-owned domains may ensure that future generations will still have at least a tamed and faded glimpse of scenes which once enchanted and inspired some of America's greatest painters, but the constant trammeling by sightseers and pilgrims as they trek along the carved-out trails only adds to the erosion, pollution and litter along the way. We sometimes diminish what we come to admire.

Accelerated change is the hallmark of the twentieth century, and the Catskills are not immune. The phenomenon of post-WWII mobility has diminished the number of hamlets and villages in the region in which a significant portion of the population shares family ties or childhood memories. When the Catskill Mountain Quilters Hall of Fame held its first induction in 1982, five of the six honorees were women who had been born in the Catskills. Only twelve years later, at the induction ceremony of 1994, all five women honored had moved to the Catskills in their adult years. They had chosen to be here.

And that may be the region's saving grace. One doesn't move to the Catskills for the climate, or to make one's fortune. One moves to the Catskills in search of a good place to call "home," and one stays because of the land and the people. The cloves, valleys and mountain hollows are peopled by individuals who are where they are because they want to be there, and somehow they make a go of it.

This gathering together of people from diverse backgrounds, but with shared or similar values, is fertile ground for art. "All are welcome" is the stated policy of every quiltmaking guild in the Catskills, and each new member who answers the call grafts her individual genius onto the tradition she encounters. It is an intricate delicate dance, a mutually-sustaining embrace where tradition joins hands with experimentation, old welcomes new, and a fine ancient art finds new expression for the varied urges welling from the modern soul.

THE UNBROKEN THREAD

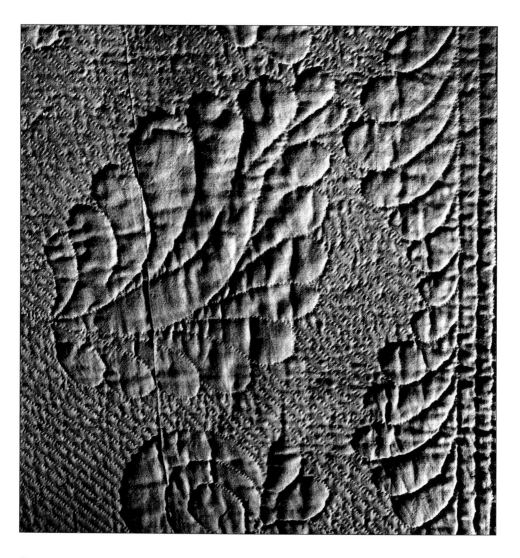

DETAIL OF A LATE-EIGHTEENTH-CENTURY/EARLY-NINETEENTH-CENTURY LINSEY-WOOLSEY WHOLECLOTH QUILT. THE QUILT IN ITS ENTIRETY MEASURES 84" BY 90" AND CONTAINS A CARDED WOOL BATTING. COLLECTION OF THE GREENE COUNTY HISTORICAL SOCIETY, BRONCK MUSEUM.

CHAPTER 2

Quiltmaking in the Catskills: The History

Most of the time I think about the lady a hundred years ago. My favorite I call 'Log Cabin Lucy.' I'll sit there and say, if I have a problem, 'How would she handle it?' After all, she never even had algebra. She did-n't even have the eighth grade education. Maybe no education at all. If she can handle it, why can't I? [Diane Atkins, quiltmaker, Liberty, 1993]

Take two pieces of fabric, sandwich between them a layer of unspun wool or cotton, then stitch the three together. Quilting is a simple concept: three separate layers closely stitched together create a warmer and more durable garment or bedcover.

If you don't have all the necessary ingredients, improvise. Dolores A. Hinson, author of *Quilting Manual*, noted:

In the past, tree bark, animal skins such as chamois, hair, leaves, moss, paper, strings, rags, game bird feathers ... have been used as quilt fillers when the more conventional fillers were unavailable. Quilts have been dated by the newspapers, love letters, political papers, and diary pages found inside them. Old clothing, sweaters, stockings, worn out quilts and even paper money have provided warmth for many persons.[1]

In the Catskill Mountains, old blankets were a popular filler during the Depression years, and several examples remain extant. They were "tied off" as "comforters" (originally: "comfortables"), necessarily; the toughness of a wool blanket discouraged the quilter's needle.

Not enough of one fabric for the top layer? Use what you have. Piecing together varied fabrics for a usable top layer created the "patchwork" quilt. Add talent, art and industry, and the design possibilities are infinite. Art is invention, and necessity often mothers them both.

Prior to the time when access to a multitude of differently colored or patterned fabrics made patchwork quilts a possibility, the designs left in the wake of the quilter's needle alone formed embellishment. These "wholecloth" quilts can be wondrous, depending on the eye and the art of the individual needlesmith—from simple cross-hatch stitching to wreaths, ferns, flowers, leaves and vines, even entire representational scenes. The Smithsonian has a quilt in its collection, made by Miss Virginia Mason Ivy of Logan County, Kentucky. It is a "white on white"—white thread stitched through plain white cloth. The needle-worker etched an elaborately-detailed realistic depiction—like a draftsman with pen and sketchboard—all in thread, titled "A Representation of the Fair Ground Near Russelville, Kentucky, 1856". According to Lenice Ingram Bacon in her book, *American Patchwork Quilts,* "The quilt measures 7 feet 8 inches long by 7 feet 3 inches wide, and there are approximately 150 stitches in every square inch. It has been calculated by authorities who have viewed the quilt that there are 1,214,352 stitches in the whole display."[2]

Quilting is hard physical work. Those million-plus stitches had to take their toll. If you visit a quilting bee, and if there is a moment's quiet (and some groups are taciturn), you will hear a constant "popping" as the needles pierce the fabrics. The popping sound testifies to the resistance offered to a needle by three layers of fabric.

> *When you start out young, your eyes give out as you get older. Arthritis gets to your hands. In quilting, as in all handsewing, there is also this critical tension. When you're doing hand-quilting, and pushing that needle up and down through all those layers, you can't push too hard. And if you don't push hard enough, the needle will not go through all the layers.*

*When I haven't quilted for a few months, the hand isn't right,
the tension. I have to work at it. After an hour or so, I'm back
in the groove again.* [Hilda Pleva, 1993]

Yet today's polyester fills allow the needle to pass through much more easily than the cotton or wool battings of the past. The Bronck House Museum, home to the Greene County Historical Society, has in its collection what is possibly the oldest surviving Catskill Mountains quilt (p. 18). It is a linsey-woolsey wholecloth quilt with a coarsely woven backing, stuffed with carded wool. The top was home-dyed a deep blue and then glazed with an egg white mixture. The textiles (homespun and home-woven) and the technique indicate an origin possibly as early as the Revolutionary War, maybe even earlier. The quilt was passed down through generations of the Bronck family but, as with most antique quilts, the maker is unknown. She could have been a member or friend of the Bronck family, or she could have been a slave. The quilt may even have not been made in the Catskills at all. It has the heft of a throw rug, yet the quilter's needle etched delicate ivy and feather patterns through all three tough heavy layers.

The quilter's art has never in the past been as widely appreciated and valued as it is today (and "valued" in every sense of the word—Sotheby's recently sold a Civil War-era quilt for $260,000.)[3] But the fact that a bedcovering has survived 200+ years indicates that fine examples were prized, though the makers remain humbly anonymous. It all seems to depend upon into whose hands the quilt was passed. The carefully-preserved Bronck House collection is missing two fine specimens of mid-nineteenth-century signature quilts, which were donated but then destroyed because they were in such poor condition. One was dated 1848 and consisted of ninety blocks, each signed by a different resident of Greenville, Coxsackie or New Baltimore. The other was a friendship album quilt inscribed "Forget Me Not 1851." It was found covering a stack of firewood, forgotten and abandoned, open to the rain, snow and bleaching sun, its plaintive inscription barely legible.

Textiles being such a fragile and perishable medium, the wonder of it is that so many antique Catskill Mountains quilts have survived. Every museum and historical society throughout the region has its own substantial collection. Most residents whose forebears had lived in the Catskills have heirloom quilts which were passed down to them. In fact, old quilts are so plentiful in the Catskills that it is not at all unusual to find an 1880s Victorian crazy quilt or a Depression-era scrap quilt offered at a yard sale for $10-$30.

As awareness increases of the value (both intrinsic and monetary) of antique quilts, more and more find their way out of closets, attics and cedar chests. When the Best House was donated to the Middleburg Public Library in 1991, perhaps no part of the contents of this stuffed-to-the-rafters rambling Victorian home created more excitement than the quilt collection. The two dozen quilts discovered exemplify nearly a century of changing styles and fabrics; it is a museum of American quiltmaking in miniature.

The house was built circa 1884 by Dr. Christopher Best, a general practitioner. The origins of the quilts remain a mystery, for only one was signed–an embroidered Victorian crazy quilt throw constructed in the early twentieth century and signed by a woman in the family. The varying styles and quality of workmanship of all the rest suggest numerous different quiltmakers, opening the possibility that they might have been rendered as payment for services performed by the good doctor–a not uncommon practice in nineteenth-century rural America.

The collection contains several utilitarian quilts which were tied off rather than quilted, made to be used not admired, a careful husbanding of scraps of fabric recombined into artless household objects. But even with these utility quilts an attempt was often made to create symmetry and design. The most interesting example in the Best House collection is a tied quilt pieced from large orange and black squares. The coarseness of the weave suggests that the material was homespun and hand-woven, and it appears to have been hand-dyed–practices we associate with pre-industrial America. But self-sufficiency in rural America did not die with the Industrial Revolution, and it is impossible to date a quilt solely on such evidence. It may have been made in the early, mid- or late 1800s, or it may be a product of the early twentieth century. Dating quilts is a tricky business and the history of quiltmaking, like history in general, is more often than not a matter of supposition and guesswork, building conclusions from a few isolated clues.

Side-by-side with these utility quilts are magnificent examples of the best of the quilter's art from several different eras. These are "show" quilts, made to be admired and treasured as heirlooms. They were probably brought out on special occasions for visitors' use or adorned spare bedrooms, or they functioned as day coverings for the family's beds and were carefully removed at night.

There is a stylized "Tulip" applique quilt in green, red and white, a pattern and color scheme popular from 1840-1900; a blue and white pieced "Northwind" design, closely quilted in leaf patterns (1830-1880); a red and white pieced "Delectable Mountains" (1840-1910); several "Mariner's Compass," with fabrics from different eras; an assortment of pieced quilts such as "Bear's Paw," "Burgoyne Surrounded," "Birds In Flight" (1850-1930); a "Log Cabin" coverlet (1860-1930); a "scrap" quilt backed with unbleached sacks advertising "5 Pounds Superior Quality Granulated Sugar, Refined by Harkmeyer & Elder, New York" (1900-1930); a pieced "Double Z," elaborately and beautifully quilted in patterns of leaves, tulips and weeping willows (1840-1890).

The Best House collection is representative of antique Catskill Mountains quilts because, unlike Hawaiian, Amish or Baltimore Album quilts, which are immediately recognizable as emblematic of a place, culture or specific time frame, quilts from the Catskills are not so easily defined or identifiable. They reflect all trends, styles and patterns, just as the people of the Catskills have never been, since earliest days, ethnically homogeneous. Close to the primary port of entry to the new world, the Catskills beckoned to each new wave of immigrants as they sought a better life for themselves and their families. Just as there is no typical Catskillian, there is no typical Catskill Mountains quilt.

Fine examples have survived of virtually every style and pattern prevalent and popular during the last two hundred years. The Museum of American Folk Art, in the course of the New York Quilt Project, an endeavor to "locate, document, preserve and create an archive for the quilts of its home state,"[4] brought many Catskill Mountains quilts to light which had been cloistered in private collections. One of the oldest was a "central medallion" quilt–featuring a large central design framed by (usually) several pieced and/or appliqued borders. Often the central design was an appliqued "Tree of Life" or a large pieced star, but in this case the design was a "Monogram Medallion"–appliqued in the center were the letters and

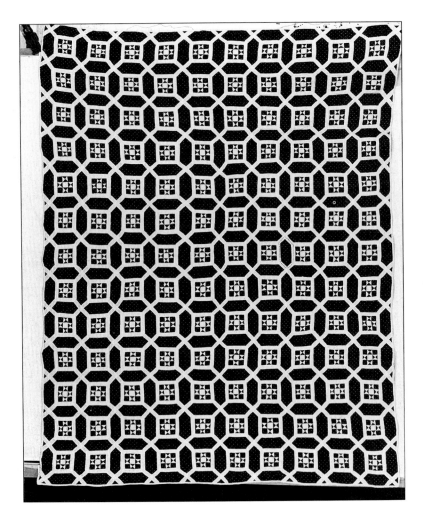

WEDDING QUILT, "OHIO STAR IN A GARDEN MAZE." FROM THE ESTATE OF RUBY GUERNSEY SCHAEFFER, THIS 72" BY 84" WEDDING QUILT WAS HAND-PIECED AND HAND-QUILTED BY FAMILY AND FRIENDS OF MS. SCHAEFFER'S GRANDMOTHER, AND THEN PRESENTED TO HER AT HER WEDDING IN SCHOHARIE IN 1844. INITIALS AND HEARTS ARE QUILTED IN WHITE THREAD THROUGHOUT THE BLUE PIECES OF THE QUILT. THE QUILT IS IN EXCELLENT CONDITION, AND MUST NEVER HAVE BEEN USED AS A BEDCOVERING. COLLECTION OF ARLENE VROOMAN.

CRIB QUILT, "OHIO STAR IN A GARDEN MAZE." FROM THE ESTATE OF RUBY GUERNSEY SCHAEFFER, THIS 35" BY 40" CRIB QUILT, FOLLOWING THE SAME PATTERN AND USING MANY OF THE SAME MATERIALS AS THE 1844 WEDDING QUILT FROM THE SAME COLLECTION, WAS MADE CIRCA 1848 IN SCHOHARIE FOR THE BIRTH OF MS. SCHAEFFER'S MOTHER. UNLIKE THE WEDDING QUILT, THIS CRIB QUILT WAS MADE TO BE USED AND SHOWS SIGNS OF WEAR AND TEAR. COLLECTION OF ARLENE VROOMAN.

numerals "H D B 1807." It was made by a member of the DuBois family of New Paltz, Ulster County.[5]

Signed and dated antique quilts are, unfortunately for the historian, a rarity—perhaps one in a hundred contains any sort of prove-
nance. But the DuBois family seems to have had a penchant for
memorializing. Carter Houck, quilt magazine editor, discovered an
"Oak Leaf" applique quilt from the same family. It was obviously a
wedding quilt: the border consists of appliqued hearts with pieced letters and numerals giving the couple's initials and the date, 1849.[6]

There is no clear line of demarcation marking the passing of one
quilt style or design method and the rise in popularity of the next, but
as the nineteenth century gained momentum "block" construction
became the overwhelming favorite, displacing the wholecloth and
central medallion quilts. Noteworthy exceptions remain, such as the
appliqued and embroidered "Tree of Life" counterpane (now in the
Smithsonian) made by an anonymous quiltmaker in Ulster County in
the mid-1800s for a Dr. Hasbrouck and his wife.[7] And the Museum of
American Folk Art catalogued a Civil War-era "white on white," the
design raised and emphasized with trapunto (extra stuffing added
between the quilting lines to give a bas-relief sculptural effect to the
surface), which was produced by Mary Anna Hill McMinn in
Davenport, Delaware County, and for which she commissioned an
artist to design and draw the quilting pattern—an unusual nineteenth-
century alliance of the fine and folk arts in the Catskills region.[8]

Block construction allowed the quiltmaker greater mobility.
Whereas the wholecloth quilts chained the quiltmaker to a large frame
for the duration of the project, the building of a quilt top "block by
block"—usually in squares of twelve to sixteen inches—meant the quiltmaker could piece or applique the sections of the top virtually anywhere she could take her sewing basket and bag of scraps. Perhaps the
greater degree of comfort afforded by this sudden freedom accounts,
at least partially, for the much greater popularity of quiltmaking in the
nineteenth century than in the eighteenth, though other factors must
be taken into consideration as well (most notably the wider availabili-
ty of factory-made materials.)

Block construction also unleashed the quiltmaker's inventiveness,
especially in regard to pieced geometric patterns. As the quiltmaker

arranged or moved around her finished blocks prior to joining them together, new patterns became apparent, and new designs developed from old standards (the elegant "Irish Chain" from the basic "Nine-Patch" is just one example.)

Many presumably nineteenth-century quilts with block construction survive and, fortunately, a small number are either dated or datable. Arlene Vrooman has a blue and white "Ohio Star in a Garden Maze," which has been carefully passed down and preserved for generations in her house in Schoharie (p.24). It is dated 1844, and inscribed with initials throughout. Arlene surmises that it was a "wedding quilt"—made for the bride-to-be prior to her wedding and initialed by her friends and family. It is in perfect condition and must never have been used (or used very sparingly). There is a little crib quilt (p.25) in the same collection which is a miniature replica of the 1844 quilt, with the same pattern and fabrics but exhibiting signs of wear and use. Together they tell a tale of rural family life a century and a half ago, a humble story told in cloth.

Another pieced block quilt, telling a different story of love and caring, is in the collection of the Pratt Museum in Greene County (p.31). It was made by Suzanna Slater for her husband, John Towner, of Athens, NY, while he was serving with the 20th State Militia during the Civil War. It features five large blue stars composed of hundreds of small diamond-shaped pieces. On each side are brown and white chevrons which resemble a sergeant's stripes. Though John never became a sergeant, he did survive the conflict, so the more important of the quiltmaker's prayers apparently was answered.

Many of the dated nineteenth-century Catskill Mountains quilts are "signature" or "album" quilts, such as the 1844 bridal quilt in the Vrooman collection. They were made for a variety of reasons—for friendship or fund-raising, as mementos or memorials—and they appear to have been immensely popular for a long span of time.

Doris West Brooks, in a recent issue of *The Hemlock,* the newsletter of the Mountain Top Historical Society of Haines Falls, Greene County, wrote of two signature quilts which were donated to the Society. The earlier one, dated "Nov. 25, 1846" and signed "Lucy J. Hains, State of NY, Hunter, Green C," appears to be a family record, containing as it does 48 names of members of the Aaron Hains family,

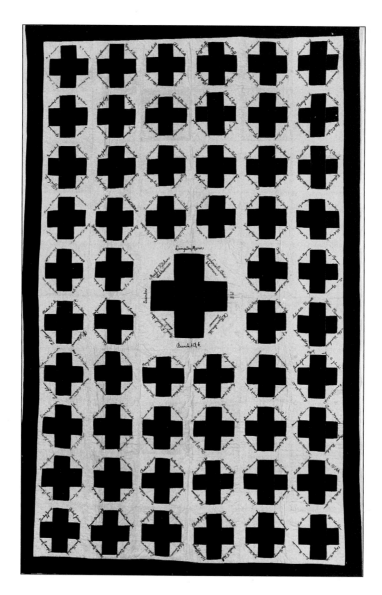

RED CROSS QUILT, 1918. THIS TWIN-SIZE FUND-RAISING QUILT WAS MACHINE-APPLIQUED AND HAND-QUILTED BY THE RED CROSS AUXILIARY OF LIVINGSTON MANOR, SULLIVAN COUNTY. DONORS WROTE THEIR SIGNATURES ON THE BLOCKS, AND THEN THE SIGNATURES WERE EMBROIDERED. COLLECTION OF THE SULLIVAN COUNTY HISTORICAL SOCIETY.

all carefully embroidered in red cross-stitch. The second appears to have been a fund-raising quilt, as it was made by the Haines Falls Ladies Aid Society. It contains 260 names embroidered on alternating red and white spokes of the "Fan" pattern which was repeated over and over in the blocks that make up the quilt. It must have been a long work-in-progress: the embroidered dates on that quilt range from 1877 to 1906.[9]

Sometimes a signature quilt was presented to an esteemed person on a significant occasion, such as the "Chimney Sweep" quilt, currently in the collection of the Sullivan County Historical Society, given to the Reverend William Ferrie and his wife by "the Women of Associated Reformed Presbyterian Church of Mongaup Valley." Whether the quilt commemorated the Reverend Ferrie joining the congregation, or departing, is not known, but he was pastor of that particular flock from 1869 until 1897.

The Sullivan County Historical Society houses another noteworthy signature quilt, a World War I fund-raising quilt made and signed by the "Red Cross Auxiliary of Livingston Manor" and dated "Dec. 1918" (p.28). This striking red and white quilt features the organization's officers' names embroidered on a central medallion consisting of a large red cross, surrounded by blocks containing smaller red crosses emblazoned with donors' signatures.

Quilts and war relief have been associated together since the Civil War when Sanitary Commission Fairs were organized throughout the northern states. They raised a total of $4,500,000 during the war years to help pay for medical supplies and the training of nurses. The fairs were organized by women and featured goods, especially quilts, handmade by women. The New York branch of the commission alone donated 26,408 quilts for sale at the fairs.[10]

How many of those were Catskill Mountains quilts? No one knows. No records remain. But it may be assumed that the Catskill Mountains, which contributed so many of her sons to the conflict, also carried its share of the burden on the home front. Almost every church throughout the region had a ladies aid society which produced goods to help support the parish, and those societies during wartime could quickly adapt their skills to the need at hand, like a National Guard of seamstresses.

The United Methodist Women of the Ashland Community Church in Greene County—who still meet, to this day, once a week to quil tops—were formerly the Ladies Sewing Circle of Mitchell Hollow. Their records reflect how the ladies responded to World War I:

Dec 5 1917 At the home of Mr. & Mrs. John Barlow 19 ladies ... met in the forenoon for the quilting. everyone worked busily untill the noon hour and two of the quilts were nearly compleated before dinner when we ajourned to the dining room where two long tables were spread with an abundance of good things ... the remaining quilt was soon tied. Many hands do make short work of it and then all were basted for the binding and stitched and the box packed. The Chairman next brought before the meeting the proposition of Sewing for the local Red-Cross and it was desided to set aside Several meeting after the Holidays for this work.

... the red Cross work has been received and a meeting was held on Dec 28th at the home of Mrs. Chittenden as we could there have the use of two sewing machines and the work would progress faster as much of it is machine work .. it was desided to send for more and give a few more meeting to this much needed work.

Jan 11th 1918 We had a good turnout & accomplished a good deal of work 4 of the ladies expressed a desire to join the Red Cross as members which will make 14 members for Mitchell Hollow.

Thursday Jan 24 The Red Cross work was finished ... We have made 9 bed shirts 12 operating leggings 6 pairs bed socks 15 triangular slings 21 comfort pillows 10 tray cloths & 5 [napkins?].

Through January 1919, as hospital transport ships steamed westward bringing home wounded Americans from Europe's battlefields, Red Cross work continues to be mentioned in the secretary's reports for the Ladies Sewing Circle.

The history of quiltmaking in the Catskills would be incomplete without further mention of the ladies aid societies. Records are scarce, missing or incomplete, but the societies seem to have been extremely prevalent in the Catskills, a part of virtually every community. They formed and congregated to support their church, the proceeds from

CIVIL WAR QUILT. THIS 76" BY 82" QUILT WAS MADE BY SUZANNA SLATER OF ATHENS, GREENE COUNTY, FOR HER HUSBAND, JOHN TOWNER, WHILE HE SERVED IN COMPANY K OF THE 20TH NEW YORK STATE MILITIA DURING THE CIVIL WAR. EACH OF THE PATRIOTIC BLUE STARS WAS SEWN TOGETHER FROM OVER 100 SMALL DIAMOND-SHAPED PIECES. COLLECTION OF THE ZADOCK PRATT MUSEUM.

their handwork helping to pay everything from the minister's salary to church repairs and improvements, new hymnals or a new church organ, or benefiting missionary work abroad. Quilts were not the only products of their hands–they made rag rugs, tablecloths, napkins, bedspreads, aprons, potholders and more–but quilts were often their mainstay, and many Catskill Mountains women had their first lessons in quiltmaking while gathered around a frame in a church hall. They were the forerunners of today's secular guilds and probably derived much of their widespread popularity by fulfilling the same social needs.

One of the earliest documented societies was the Roses Brook Methodist Church Ladies Missionary Group in Stamford, Delaware County. One of their products remains extant, a blue and white "Blazing Star," pieced and appliqued by Sarah Permelia Peck (b. 1814), quilted by the ladies and dated 1845.[11]

The societies would either "quilt for hire" and donate the fee to the church (as the Claryville Ladies Aid Society and the United Methodist Women in Ashland still do to this day), or they would construct their own quilts from scratch and either send them to missions or sell them at home and send the proceeds to the missions, as The Women's Missionary Society of the North Kortright Presbyterian Church (Delaware County) did from 1891 continuously until 1973, when the group finally disbanded because there were no longer enough members.[12]

Aside from holding a raffle or selling their quilts at church fairs, another popular method used by the societies to profit from their quilt-making was to make a signature quilt. The Meridale Presbyterian Ladies Aid Society (also Delaware County), which has been making fund-raising quilts since the turn of the century, pieced and quilted a "Grandmother's Flower Garden" in 1979 and then sold the right to area residents to have their names embroidered thereon for $1.00 apiece.[13] Often, with a signature quilt, the names are then pooled, one name is drawn, and the winner is presented with the quilt.

Another such quilt is currently in the collection of the Bronck House Museum in Coxsackie. It was made by the Ladies Union of the First Baptist Church in Catskill (Greene County) in 1905. It features a simple design of alternating red and white triangles, and was tied

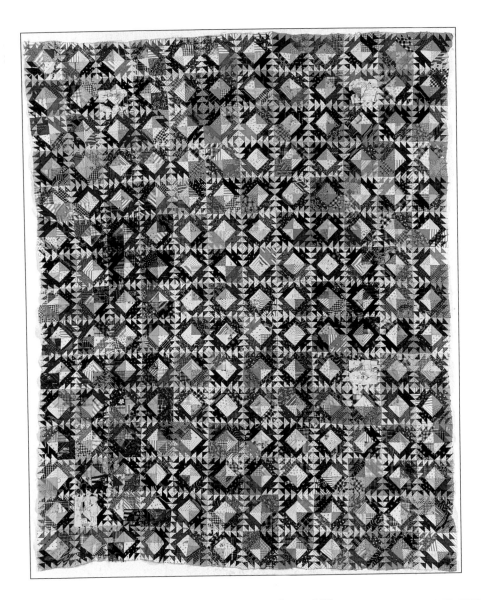

"LOST SHIP." DATING FROM 1893, THIS 63" BY 80" UNQUILTED PIECED TOP MAY HAVE BEEN ENTERED IN COMPETITION AT A COUNTY FAIR, BECAUSE SEWN TO THE BACK IN FOUR DIFFERENT SPOTS ARE LABELS WITH THE LEGEND: "'LOST SHIP' BY FRANKIE DRUM, AGE 13, BIG HOLLOW, CONTAINS 8,640 PIECES." COLLECTION OF THE ZADOCK PRATT MUSEUM.

instead of quilted. Each of the hundreds of triangles features a different name, a privilege which cost each donor 10 cents.

Many ladies aid societies have come and gone in the Catskills, leaving no records behind and little to remember them by but the recollections of a few area residents. In service to their communities and their churches, they helped continue and foster an unbroken tradition of quiltmaking right up to the present day. But the Ladies Sewing Circle of Mitchell Hollow has left us with a fairly detailed report of their meetings from 1915 through 1928, and perhaps we may extrapolate from that record a glimpse into the lives and works of the generations of Catskill Mountains women who donated their time and labor throughout the entire region for well over a century and a half. It is a fascinating glimpse of mountaintop life in the early twentieth century:

The 19 day of Feb. [1915] proved to be pleasant and a goodly number of ladies and young people gathered at Mrs. Austins for the quilting. We got together rather early two quilts were tied before dinner. Then dinner being announced we all left our work to do justice to the meal prepared for us. I think we really did enjoy the dinner all seasoned with a good laugh there were 30 in all 14 ladies 13 young people & 3 men. then we went to work and tied 2 more quilts About 4:30 the party broke up leaving a few working at the last quilt.

October 8th 1915 the ladies met with Mrs Lucy Chittenden to begin our usual missionary work: 12 ladies were there. Some worked at little underclothes and others did piecing. We were entertained by a flat-iron agent a good share of the afternoon. A good talker.

16 ladies were present at the quilting Wednesday Nov 17 We had two quilts to tie & finish then pack the box to be sent to the "The Home of the Friendless" New York (we valued the box at 20 dollars. credit given the L. S. Society)

Friday Jan 28, 1916 "Sec." account. Paid of the following.
13 yds calico 4.47
Caring for Chapel 3.33
Inshurence on Chapel $10.13
Mrs Lucy Chittenden quilt lining. 49
Mrs. R. W. Howard quilt lining etc 2.01
Mr Markarian Salery (Nov) 8.50 paid for having organ cleaned 3.00

Victorian crazy quilt, 1890. This 60" by 70" unquilted silk "throw" was made in Schoharie County, maker unknown. It is a veritable "sampler" of embroidery stitches. Collection of Christine Polak.

A 1916 (undated) entry discusses the annual summer church fair, to which the ladies contributed "aprons, linen handkerchiefs, piecing, and babyclothes." The various booths were listed: candy booth, ice cream, grab bag, and one titled "fancy articles." The entry ends with: "Our fair netted us $59.67 ... We went home very tired but well paid for our work."

Thursday Feb. 17 - 11 ladies met with Mrs. Gordon it was a beautiful day. And all enjoyed the delightful sleigh ride going and coming.

Friday afternoon - March 22 [1918] *We were treated to warm maple sugar. the first of the season.*

March 6 [1919] *We met with Mrs. H. B. Maben for the quilting. we had the best turn out yet 31 of us enjoyed the spread planned & carried out by our quilt committee this completes our all day meetings for a time as the busy season approaches.*

March 22 Bad roads & sugar making interfere now. so our meetings will be called off for awhile.

The opening meeting in May ... This time 7 ladies were present we took up the work with better courage to get something accomplished before strawberry time.

Oct ... we planned to make one large & one small comfort quilt out of the white bags together with any good second hand clothing that might be given to send to a Ministers family in Carolina. The next week we will meet with Addie & tie the quilt ... we each contributed 50 cts apiece to by cotton silkateen etc.

Jan 29 [1920] *at Mrs. Mabens there were 9 of us present. We sewed & sewed rags all day* [for rag rugs].

March 4th We met to work at making a candlewick bedspread. this was new work for the most of us.

Jan 14 [1921] *Received check for bedspread $12.*

At this quilting party Jan 21 there were 9 ladies were present One quilt was given to Our Society by Mrs Lucy Chittenden for the fair. the other one was ordered by a city party Our dinner consisted of beef & mashed potato with gravy squash scalloped corn salad pickles hot rolls cake & coffee.

Jan 28 [1922] *voted to help on Ministers salary if necessary.*

Jan 25 [1923] *The day was spent in piecing a blue & white quilt.*

General report for the year 1922. Our work has been unusually successful the past year having so many orders for bedding from city parties consisting of three bedspreads three bolsters three quilts which brought us $84 dollars.

Fri. Feb. 6, 1925 There we are back on our old job again quilting on the basket quilt, cuting out blocks for another & sewing rags.

March 19, 1926 It was a beautiful day and they turned out good there were 18 Ladies present 4 from Windham. some of the ladies behaved very bad but they worked good and we hope to have another meeting like that soon.

Nov. 4, 1927 We done quite a little on the quilt.

Jan 26, 1928 Our first meeting since the Holidays We put on double Irish chain quilt [which was finished in three meetings].

Mar. 15, 1928 We finish crib quilt and worked on basket quilt and put on another quilt for Mrs Olive Converting to be quilted.

The entries end that year, but the Society carried on. Whatever subsequent records they kept, if any, have been lost. Similarly, the first entry for 1913 gives no indication that this was a newly-formed organization; it begins in medias res. No one knows for certain when the Ladies Sewing Circle of Mitchell Hollow first began, but it may confidently be assumed that its roots extend well back into the nineteenth century. The diary from 1913 to 1928 is a small window opened briefly on the past. The various ladies aid societies throughout the Catskills were humble organizations, quietly going about their work in near-anonymity.

Following the Civil War, new quilt styles and patterns began to emerge. One of the most popular of these, a perennial favorite to this day, is the "Log Cabin" design. It was most frequently tied-off as a comforter, largely because the most common material for the top was heavy wool, but exceptions remain, such as the Victorian (silk) "Log Cabin" quilted by Mrs. John P. Van Valkenbergh of Halcott (Greene County) circa 1915.[14]

The latter half of the nineteenth century saw the advent of the "crazy quilt" fad (p.35), which swept the Catskills along with the rest

"1876 Centennial Quilt." This 69" by 79" quilt, made in Delaware County, contains pieced, appliqued and embroidered patterns and symbols, and is the only extant quilt made in 1876 in the Catskills to celebrate the nation's centennial. Makers unknown. Collection of the Delaware County Historical Association.

"1976 Bicentennial Quilt." Made in Delaware County for the bicentennial, this 75" by 96" quilt, like the centennial quilt of 100 years earlier, contains piecing, applique and embroidery, but unlike the earlier quilt, it exhibits the late-twentieth-century penchant for pictorial quilts. The names of 114 county residents who worked on the quilt are inscribed on the back. Collection of the Delaware County Historical Association.

of the country. The crazy quilts were usually not quilts per se; they were "throws," consisting of only two layers, sometimes just one, and they were very, very rarely quilted. They were almost exclusively decorative, meant to be draped over a sofa or a piano, an artful display of the maker's fine silks and embroidery skills. But since the top layer was pieced together of many different materials, the term "quilt" was applied.

Quilt magazine editor Carter Houck stated that "Candace Wheeler was almost single-handedly responsible for the crazy quilt fad in America." Candace, together with Louis Comfort Tiffany, had founded the first chapter of the Decorative Arts Society in New York in 1876, an outgrowth of the Decorative Arts Movement in England which was inspired by the works and writings of William Morris and John Ruskin—essentially a revolt against the factory-made household goods of the Industrial Revolution. Candace Wheeler, who has been called "the first and foremost textile designer of the nineteenth century,"[15] also helped found the New York Women's Exchange in 1878, an outlet for artistic women to sell their wares. In later years, she helped form the Associated American Artists, an experimental design company for interior decorators. Her influence on home decoration in the late nineteenth century was pervasive and profound.

Candace was born in Delhi, Delaware County, in 1827. Although most of her adult life was spent in New York City, she began to spend her summers in the Catskills beginning in 1883, purchasing a cottage just outside of Tannersville, Greene County, in what would eventually become the site of the Onteora Club—originally, in Candace's time, an arts colony, in later years an enclave of the well-to-do.

It is hard to assess Candace Wheeler's specific impact upon her native Catskills. Crazy quilts abound in museums and private collections throughout the region, but they do not appear to be much more prevalent here than elsewhere in the country. The Onteora Club (in the 1880s called "Lotus Land" by Candace) has always been somewhat cloistered from the general community. But the Club, since its inception, has also been an important source of employment for the local population, and no doubt the cooks and housekeepers returned to their farmhouses in Jewett or Maplecrest inspired by furnishings and needlework displays they had seen in the Onteora "cottages."

The trademarks of the crazy quilts are asymmetry and decorative embroidery, and the most popular materials were silk, satin and velvet although, as always with quilts, exceptions abound. Some Catskill Mountains crazy quilts, for example, employed wool materials for the top.

A visit to the Old Stone Fort Museum in Schoharie, home of the Schoharie County Historical Society, will reward the quilt enthusiast with a glimpse of one of the finest specimens of the genre, a crazy quilt throw in brilliant red silks made by Caroline Ward of Dormansville (undated). Nearly every piece of the hundreds of fabric scraps which comprise the top exhibits a different embroidered wildflower, butterfly, bird or animal. It is a tour de force of the embroiderer's art, a visual catalog of the flora and fauna of upstate New York.

Another fad that started in the late nineteenth century was to assemble a quilt top using as many pieces as possible. The Pratt Museum has an unquilted top, titled "Lost Ship" (p.33), made in 1893 and signed by "Miss Frankie Drum, Big Hollow" (today's Maplecrest, Greene County). Frankie proudly added on the legend that the top contains 8,640 pieces. She was thirteen years old at the time the top was completed.

A later development, similar in theme (and still popular in the Catskills into the 1990s), is the "charm quilt"–a top of many pieces wherein each piece is from a different fabric, with no two pieces alike, a mind-boggling (and one would think, tedious) achievement.

The extravagance and prodigality of the Victorian and Georgian eras gave way to the Great Depression when, suddenly, any fabric was prized. Quiltmakers in the Catskills, as elsewhere throughout the country, resorted to using flour sacks, sugar bags and feed sacks for quilt backings, as well as for sheets, aprons—even dresses. Nothing was wasted, and the makers of the cloth containers responded to the national mood by replacing the plain white bags with colorful prints.

The Depression is remembered well by many quiltmakers still active in the Catskills:

> [We] *used to boil it* [feedbags] *in bleach on the stove to get the logos out ... When we got the logos out, four of them made sheets. I was so glad when I got married that I didn't have to have those sheets, because where those sheets came together in*

the middle was a big hard spot which never washed away. We made everything out of feedbags. [Beatrice Rexford, Sullivan County]

What a treat to accompany my father when he purchased feed! We got to choose the print, and to look for duplicates—so you could make a "full" skirt. [Grace McMullen, Ulster County, remembering her childhood in Illinois]

Marie Genthner of Saugerties, Ulster County, who grew up in a baker's family during the Depression, remembers the supply side of this famous chapter in American home economics:

When we had so many flour bags, years ago, we used to fold 'em up and tie 'em in dozens and sell 'em for fifty cents a dozen. Because flour came in flour bags, not paper bags. It was muslin—a heavy grade of muslin. And sugar came in a lighter weight. And then the farmers got chicken feed in prints—tiny prints that ladies used to make aprons out of, and children's clothes ... they used to make sheets and pillow cases out of 'em. And we used to find they made excellent dish towels. Fifty cents a dozen. Didn't wash 'em or anything. We had the corner in the store there where they could help themselves.

Quiltmaking boomed during the Depression years as American women made a virtue of necessity, and the time-honored "waste not, want not" philosophy of the patchworker became the nation's standard. By 1934, more than 400 newspapers carried regular columns on quiltmaking.[16] Phyllis Cameron of Delaware County still has her mother's collection of Depression-era magazines, including *Ladies Home Journal, Good Housekeeping, American Agriculturist* and *Farm Journal*—all of which advertise mail-order quilt patterns for as little as ten cents apiece. And when Sears Roebuck sponsored a quilt contest in 1933, 25,000 quilts were entered at regional Sears outlets, all vying for the grand prize of $1200.[17]

The social revolution in America which began with the onset of World War II effectively ended the quilt craze that had been nurtured by the Depression, and quiltmaking went into a long decline. Wartime fabric and paper shortages hastened the decline, but the more important factor involved was the thrusting of women into the workplace where their dual role as provider and housekeeper left little leisure for anything as slow and time-consuming as quiltmaking.

Quiltmaking receded into a few isolated communities, like the Amish in Pennsylvania and Ohio, or ancestral homesteads in the Appalachians ... or a few individuals and church organizations in the Catskills.

The 1950s and 1960s—the nadir of quiltmaking in America—found the Claryville Ladies Aid Society in Sullivan County busily continuing their work as though nothing had changed. The minutes from their "Secretary's Report" read like documents from thirty years before:

1/5/54 [received a] *letter from Kentucky Mountain House at Annville Ky. for box, containing 6 yds outing, 20 flour sacks 100 lb size, and 2 mechanical pencils ... Work accomplished was putting on frames and start quilting a quilt ....*

February 20, 1962 Mrs. Lewis Van Sickle gave quilt top material and blanket for inner lining to our Aid.

Jan. 22nd 1969 Finished seventh quilt for this year already.

May 20, 1970 Worked on quilting one quilt and tied other one.

Even the value of the dollar seems not to have changed:

... we had oyster supper for church on Jan 15th [1954]. *Twenty-five (25) present. Coll. $19.40 expenses $11.30 cleared $8.10.*

January 10, 1961 A quilted quilt (top being pieced by Mrs. Henry Dulloway last year) was raffled off by chances— money realized $35.75 ...

March 14, 1961 Day gathering. began quilting on quilt belonging to Ladies Aid. Lena Slater piecing the top. Quilt to be for sale at our annual Church Fair in July ... Voted to give both Town of Demming and Town of Neversink Three dollars ($3.00) each for Red Cross.

December 17, 1963 Christmas party, exchange of gifts ($00.50 ones).

What had changed, apparently, in the intervening years since the Ladies Sewing Circle of Mitchell Hollow, was a greater interest in and awareness of pattern names. The records of the Ladies Sewing Circle rarely refer to a quilt by its pattern name; instead, the entry will refer to "the blue & white quilt" or "the pink and white quilt." The records of the Claryville ladies, however, read more like a quilt pattern encyclopedia. Among their works they list by name during the 1950s and

1960s are "Lone Star," "broken Star," "double Irish chain," "cherry quilt," "sunshine and shadows," "double wrench," "nine block," "dasher block," "butterfly quilt," "double T," "necktie," "bowtie," "Drunkard's Path," "Log Cabin," "Tree of Life," and "flat Iron."

The proliferation of patterns, and the popularity of pattern names, was a direct outgrowth of the magazine advertisements and newspaper columns of the 1920s and 1930s, although many of the patterns themselves pre-date the twentieth century.

Aside from the church societies, quiltmaking in the Catskills was also continued and carried forward by a few individuals working on their own. Later on, in the mid-1970s, when Nancy Smith put an ad in a newspaper advertising the formation of a quilting guild in Pine Hill, Ulster County, she was surprised by the extent of the response and the level of quiltmaking expertise still available. It was far from the "dead" art many presumed it to be, although the most active practitioners did, at that time, tend to be almost exclusively elderly.

Quiltmaking had survived in the Catskills for a number of reasons. Although they are now fast disappearing, ancestral family farms were still quite prevalent during the middle years of the century. Children learned from their parents and grandparents the skills they needed to run the farm and manage the household. A certain measure of self-sufficiency was required as money was hard to come by and the nearest stores could be a considerable distance away. Organizations such as the Cornell Cooperative Extension and 4-H were very active in the region, teaching a wide range of do-it-yourself skills. It would have been more unusual for a young girl growing up in the mid-twentieth-century Catskill Mountains to not know how to sew, than to be illiterate.

So the skills were already in place, and enough experienced quiltmakers were still practicing their art in the Catskills, when a combination of events led to a renaissance in appreciation of quilts which started to sweep the nation in the 1970s.

First, the Whitney Museum of American Art in New York staged an exhibition in 1971 titled "Abstract Design in American Quilts," which led to widespread recognition, perhaps for the first time, of the quilt as fine art. This came at a time when an arts and crafts revival was already gathering full steam across the country.

Then the American Bicentennial in 1976 awakened further interest in traditional crafts and customs, and women gathered together to express their patriotism and pride by creating quilts depicting the history of their communities (pp. 38, 39). For many women, this was their first taste of quiltmaking, and the communal experience they shared constructing their bicentennial quilt so closely knit them together that they continued to meet on a regular basis and eventually formed a quiltmaking guild.

Guilds sprang up seemingly overnight in communities throughout the Catskills, growing in number each year. The Patchworkers of East Jewett, Greene County, was the first, in 1973, but many others soon followed: Calico Geese (Liberty, Sullivan County), Wiltwyck (after Peter Stuyvesant's original name [meaning "wild place"] for Kingston, Ulster County), Delaware County Town and Country Quilt Guild (Delhi), Schoharie Valley Piecemakers Quilt Guild—to name but a few of the larger organizations. Some guilds grew so large that they encouraged members to create new smaller groups as sister guilds.

The membership sometimes outgrew the meeting place, as Arlene Vrooman remembers from the early days of the Schoharie Valley Piecemakers: "they were sitting two to three on a chair." And their enthusiasm is perhaps best summed up by Florence Tyler as she spoke of an intimate little group she started, the Gabbing and Laughing Society (GALS) of Delhi: "What bugs me is taking so long for lunch. I want to get back to work."

The guilds function as quiltmaking academies. The largest guilds feature formal workshops and attract guest speakers, while the smaller groups share their skills and knowledge more informally. Like their counterparts (and forerunners), the ladies aid societies, much of their activity is charitable, benefiting everything from libraries, colleges and battered women's shelters, to little leagues, volunteer fire companies and rest homes.

They are non-denominational, ethnically diverse and democratic. Over and over I was told in answer to my question about new members, "All are welcome."

The phenomenal growth in the art of quiltmaking in the Catskill Mountains the past twenty years has been repeated all across the country. With growth has come change:

*Twenty years ago, when I started quilting, it was a stan-
dard ruler, needle, thread, a yardstick—all very standard stuff.
Not anymore. We have graphed plexiglass rulers. We have
rotary cutters with self-healing board like architect's tables used
to be topped with. The books on "How To ... " have proliferated. The variety of fabric over the years. We have designers now
who work for fabric companies who exclusively design prints
for quilting. There are braces for the hands, for the strain that
occurs of doing the same actions for a long period of time. Not
to mention, you can construct a quilt on your home computer,
rent videotape lessons or watch PBS programs. There are charts
to tell you how much yardage you will need for so many
squares.* [Hilda Pleva]

One change that is not so welcome is commercial exploitation and
the pitiless mechanics of the multinational economy. If you want to
raise the hackles of a Catskills Mountain quiltmaker, mention
"Chinese quilts." They seem to be everywhere, and they are so inexpensive that American quiltmakers simply cannot compete.

Ironically, it all started with that bastion of American culture, the
Smithsonian Institute's National Museum of American History. When
the Smithsonian decided to license the rights to reproduce four nineteenth-century quilt designs from its collection to an entrepreneurial
company, American Pacific Enterprises (which then had the quilts
reproduced in China),[18] it struck a blow against contemporary
American quiltmakers, many of whom, in the Catskills and elsewhere,
had relied upon their quiltmaking to supplement their income.

American quiltmakers are furious. As Vivian Ruoff of East Jewett
said, "It's [Quiltmaking is] an American thing. We feel it belongs to
us." A letter campaign was instituted, the American Quilt Defense
Fund was formed, and quilters even marched on the Smithsonian—
with some success. In 1993, the Smithsonian agreed to limit the number of quilts produced overseas and to license American quiltmakers
to reproduce patterns from its collection.[19]

But the damage has been done. There are thousands of China-
made reproductions of classic American quilts for sale at bargain
prices in chain retail outlets across America. An American quiltmaker
can barely purchase the raw materials to make a quilt for the price
these finished quilts sell for. With their market eroded, American quilt-

makers are making fewer quilts, and the quiltmaking renaissance is now in decline. Even before the Smithsonian debacle, when American quilt prices peaked, the quiltmaker was not amply rewarded for the hundreds of hours of labor that went into each quilt. As Peg Barnes of Arkville, Delaware County, remarked: "If they ever paid a quilter by the hour, you'd never be able to afford a quilt."

Catskill Mountains quiltmakers continue to produce their remarkable art out of love for the medium, and regardless of what the future may hold for the market, it is doubtful that the "quilt craze" of the past twenty years will soon pass. What remains disturbing is how the quiltmakers of the Catskills labor on in relative obscurity, and how those among them who struggle to make ends meet in order to continue their art suffer from this neglect.

> *It's always been a mystery to me. Look what happened in Appalachia* [the highly organized, economically successful Mountain Artisans collective, spearheaded by Nancy Rockefeller]. *And I've always wondered: Why can't anybody come to the Catskills and do that for the quilters and the people up there? I mean, we're trying to do it in this area* [Kingston] *right now, with the crafters. They're coming out of the woodwork—talent like you wouldn't believe. But no market for it. Same old thing for the quilters. And it's too bad ... You just can't seem to connect the two somehow.* [Nancy Smith, quiltmaker, Ulster County, 1993]

"Celebrating the Path I Followed" by Betty Verhoeven. This 72" by 86" bed quilt was hand-pieced, hand-appliqued and hand-quilted by Betty in 1992, from an original design by her daughter Johanna.

CHAPTER 3

The Catskill Mountain Quilters Hall of Fame

I *just felt there were so many real, I mean, aging ladies in there and they'd never been recognized. And it just seemed such a shame, you know? They were farmer's wives, and their husbands had passed away, but their quilting was a lifelong thing with them. And a way of life. I mean they had to do it, in the beginning. And I just felt that there was a Baseball Hall of Fame, and every kind of Hall of Fame you can think of, why not a Quilters Hall of Fame?*
[Nancy Smith, founder]

Everything that man constructs–every building, every highway, every work of art, every institution–is born when an idea begins to form and grow in the mind of one individual. Inspired by the women who joined with her and gathered around the quilt frame at the Erpf Catskill Cultural Center to form the Catskill Mountain Quilters Guild, Nancy Smith took this idea of a Quilters Hall of Fame to her friends, Bertha Mayes and Lena Johnson, and in the spring of 1982 they went to work.

They began by writing letters outlining their plan to the various guilds throughout the Catskills, asking each guild to spread the word.

49

Gradually a coalition began to form, and on July 14, 1982, the first meeting was held at the Erpf Center. A fourteen-member board of directors was established with representatives from Greene, Ulster, Sullivan and Delaware Counties (Schoharie County joined the following year), and officers were elected. Fittingly enough, Nancy Smith was the first elected president of the newly-formed Catskill Mountain Quilters Hall of Fame.

The first items on the agenda were to formulate a nomination procedure and establish criteria for the selection of the inductees from those nominated. It was decided that candidates would apply directly to a member of the board of directors, and that member would then sponsor the candidate before the entire board. After the presentation by the sponsor, the entire board would vote and the decision was made. In those early days of the selection process, a candidate or sponsor did not have to present samples of the candidate's work.

The criteria upon which the board made its decision included originality, workmanship and the "contribution made to quilting and other quilters." Sharing skills and knowledge to help propagate and advance the art of quilting was an important consideration for selection from the start. Gender was not. In the open-hearted tradition for which quilters are renowned, men were invited to apply. Nominees had to be legal residents of one of the four participating counties, and had to have been active in quiltmaking for a minimum of ten years. It was not necessary to be currently active.

The applications started to pour in, and the ever-difficult process of selection began. By 1982, hundreds—perhaps thousands—of quilters were plying their art in the Catskills. New guilds were forming every year to take their place side-by-side with the many time-honored and still-active church societies. Out of this wonderful abundance of talent, how do you select and separate those special few to honor among their peers? How do you say "no" to the others?

The fourteen women on the board of directors agonized over this problem as they sifted through the applications and debated the qualifications of each nominee. But the very nature of any special award and recognition dictates that a selection must be made. For every individual honored, many are passed over. In October of 1982, in a ceremony at the Erpf Catskill Cultural Center in Arkville, Bertha Ackerly,

Ruth Culver, Evadine Garrison, Nina Haynes, Madeline Sanford and Amelia White became the first six inductees into the Catskill Mountain Quilters Hall of Fame. Nancy Smith's idea had become reality, and a brand new institution was born "to honor our quilters and preserve samples of their work."

* * *

I remember one time Nancy [Smith] *and I met over in the Lexington Hotel, just her and I one night, to plan a meeting. It's so complicated now. Then it was so simple. But I guess it's got to be if it's going to mean anything.* [Vivian Ruoff, original board member]

From those tentative beginnings, the Catskill Mountain Quilters Hall of Fame has grown to an organization with over twenty contributing and participating guilds, with a combined membership of over 500 active quiltmakers from almost every town, hamlet and isolated mountain hollow of the five counties of Schoharie, Greene, Sullivan, Delaware and Ulster. It has become virtually an umbrella organization, and has been instrumental in helping to facilitate what has become a regional network of quilters. The collective virtuosity and productivity of this burgeoning community of quilters makes the Catskill Mountains a world center for the art.

There are now 46 women who have been honored by their peers with induction into the Catskill Mountain Quilters Hall of Fame. Their stories appear on the following pages.

The Hall of Fame has undergone the growing pains of any new and original organization. There have been minor controversies and disappointments. They are still in search of a site for the permanent display of the quilt blocks each inductee makes upon being selected. Two of Nancy Smith's hoped-for goals have not yet been realized: to purchase one quilt from each inductee to establish an archive and museum, and to then further recognize the honoree by registering the quilt with the National Quilt Register.

And the selection process has changed over the years. The age of the nominee is no longer an important consideration, nor is the number of years devoted to quiltmaking any longer a primary factor, although, all things else being equal, an eighty-year-old who has practiced the art since childhood would probably get the nod over a thirty-five-year-old of comparable ability who has been quilting for five or ten years. And rightly so: there is always next year.

Furtherance of the art through teaching, and contributing to the larger community unselfishly through quilt-related projects, though important from the outset, has loomed larger in the selection process as the Hall of Fame refines its aims and ideals. For a number of years, the newsletter of the Hall of Fame, when listing the criteria for selection, made it appear almost mandatory that a nominee be a member of a guild, but letters from more recent years omit that stipulation. Active participation in a guild is certainly considered an indication of dedication to the art, but it is not necessary for selection. Other factors can balance the scales.

Since 1985, the nominating process has been carried on without the nominee's participation or knowledge thereof. It is thought that, by keeping the nomination a secret from the nominee, feelings are spared should the nominee not be selected. The obverse of that debate is the difficulty of viewing the nominees' best work without their cooperation. The debate goes on. But the best efforts of the organization have been devoted to finding a selection process which is balanced and fair, and which brings to the fore the most deserving quiltmakers and the art they have produced.

In 1988, the decision was made to hold biennial elections, rather than coninue with annual inductions.

From the booklet distributed for the 1992 induction ceremony comes the following, which has become the current credo of the organization:

> *The Catskill Mountain Quilters Hall of Fame was conceived as a tribute to honor quilters who have shown dedication to the art of quiltmaking. The people chosen for a place in the Hall of Fame have perfected their design techniques, quality control and workmanship while contributing to the art of quiltmaking through the number of quilts completed. Sharing their art and caring for others is an important facet of their personality.*

The Hall of Fame today is no longer composed of the aging rural wives, quilting away in isolation and obscurity, who first inspired

Nancy Smith in 1982. In the following pages you will find some farmer's wives and widows, some of them quite elderly with ancestral roots which go back six or seven generations in the Catskills. But you will also find professional women, women in their forties, women who moved from other states or from other countries, for the Catskills continue to be a paradigm for the country as a whole: it is a melting pot in miniature.

The Catskill Mountain Quilters Hall of Fame
LIST OF INDUCTEES

1982	1985	1990
Bertha Ackerly	Marie Genthner	Virginia Hull
Ruth Culver	Hilda Pleva	Pauline Lawrence
Evadine Garrison		Mary Lowe
Nina Haynes		Christine Polak
Madeline Sanford	1986	Connie Stangel
Amelia White	Marilyn Guy	Theresa Scheetz
	Wanda Lanzi	
	Evelyn Nabors	
1983	Viola Scranton	1992
Martha Denman	Nancy Smith	Diane Atkins
Edna Moore		Peg Barnes
Virginia Roberts		Phyllis Cameron
Elsa Sanford	1987	Lois Gould
	Jeannette Hunt	Bea Rexford
	Kathy Mouser	Betty Verhoeven
1984	Vivian Ruoff	
Eleanor Faulkner	Anna Marie Tucker	
Ethel Hinkley	Arlene Vrooman	1994
Emma Kelly		Vija Clark
Agnes Proper		Janice Dayton
Kathleen Rolfs	1988	Dessa Hague
	Astrid Ormiston	Marie Kremer
	Florence Tyler	Helen Quinn

"North Carolina Lily" by Chris Polak. Machine-pieced and hand-quilted by Chris as a wedding gift for her brother John and his wife Ann, who live in North Carolina. It was completed in 1992.

CHAPTER 4

Ulster County

he most cosmopolitan county in the Catskills, Ulster features the region's only city (Kingston) and the world-famous village of Woodstock. Woodstock, of course, became famous for something that did not happen there twice (the music festivals of 1969 and 1994), but it had long before acquired a reputation for harboring and nurturing artists in every medium. Bob Dylan may be the most famous ex-resident of Woodstock, but the village's renown as an artists' "colony" extends well back into the middle of the nineteenth century. Other Catskills counties feature community colleges or trade and technical institutes, but Ulster has the only four-year full-curriculum university (SUNY New Paltz).

Ulster is certainly the most varied of the five counties. Its southern tier is within commuting range of New York City, and real estate values reflect that fact. Relatively densely populated along its 50-mile expanse of Hudson River shoreline, the western reaches are comparatively uninhabited, almost virgin territory. It is the most industrial county, but is home to the highest peak (Slide Mountain) and the largest of the manmade lakes (Ashokan Reservoir). In the small microcosm of the Catskills, it is the land of contrasts.

In the 1600s, the Dutch established several footholds in Ulster along the Hudson River, the largest and most important of which was renamed "Kingston" when the English took control of the colony. Then they burned it during the Revolution, but the colonists, showing no hard feelings (or at least an insensitivity to nomenclature), retained the name anyway.

Kingston, for a time, rivaled Albany as the upstate political and commercial center, but the relocation of the state capital from Kingston to Albany, and then the building of the Erie Canal, effectively ended the competition. Today's spreading Capital District dwarfs the little river port city, but had events turned the other way, most likely the rewards of influence and expansion could not compensate for having politicians living in your neighborhood.

Ruth Culver (b. 1922)

THE 32" BY 32" WALL-HANGING, "AMISH NINE-PATCH," WAS MACHINE-PIECED AND HAND-QUILTED BY RUTH IN 1984. IT IS A ONE-QUARTER REPRODUCTION OF A QUILT FROM *PIECED QUILTS*, BY JONATHAN HOLSTEIN.

*I*n the Catskills today there are hundreds of fine practitioners of the art of quiltmaking. There might well be far fewer had not Ruth Culver's travels around the world with her husband–a career man in the U.S. Navy–landed her in Kingston in 1958. Ruth often speaks of quiltmaking as "caring and sharing," and she has shared herself and her knowledge of the art by nurturing the skills of countless students.

Born in the small community of Lake Elsinore, California, in 1922, Ruth was raised in a tradition of quiltmaking which her mother had brought with her from the mountains of Virginia. By the age of five, Ruth had already learned to piece quilt tops, and soon after she was taught to applique. She would help her mother and her Aunt Lucy tie the "everyday" quilts; "We had these quilts that weren't necessarily what you see in quilt shows," Ruth recalls. "They were more 'utility quilts.' Although we had some good quilts that you put on when you had company." Some of those "good quilts" were quilted, "but I was never allowed to quilt," Ruth added. "I assume they thought my stitches were too big."

As Ruth looks back on her childhood during the Depression, quiltmaking was hardly considered the art that it is today: "I felt very poor because we had quilts, because by that time people had blankets. When I was eighteen, one of the first things I did when I got a job was buy my mother a blanket." For children of the Depression, that early disdain of the art is not uncommon. Quilts on the beds meant that you were too poor to shop for your bedcoverings. For those families who made quilts out of necessity, quiltmaking was as commonplace and routine–and probably as tedious–as mending clothes or canning food.

Consequently, it was many years before Ruth Culver returned to quiltmaking, and even then it was with some reluctance. In 1972, while Ruth was taking a course at Ulster County Community College, her instructor was intrigued to learn that Ruth knew how to quilt–it seemed such an arcane skill to have at that time in a city like Kingston. He urged her to approach the Department of Continuing Education with the proposal of teaching a course in quiltmaking. "I thought it was ridiculous that anyone would pay to learn how to quilt," Ruth said. But the college liked the idea, and the course was added to the curriculum that fall.

To prepare herself for the role of teacher, Ruth traveled that summer to Kutztown, Pennsylvania, for the annual Independence Day fair: "They have all these quilts in their Quilt Barn that they sell," she explained. "There were nine hundred the year I was there. And there were two groups of ladies who were around a big quilt frame, and I just sat down and watched them quilt. Then I came home and practiced." The course began that fall of 1973, and to Ruth's surprise it was well—and enthusiastically—attended.

The course became a permanent part of the curriculum, and out of those classes grew the idea for making a bicentennial quilt for Ulster County. Ruth originally planned thirty blocks, with each block depicting a different scene from Ulster County's past, but since forty-two women wanted to participate, twelve blocks were added to the design. The finished quilt measures 96 x 108 inches, with forty-two twelve-inch-square blocks. It was displayed at the college for an entire month during the bicentennial year, and hundreds of people came to see it every day. "It was the biggest attendance they had ever had," Ruth said. That quilt is now on permanent display in the college library.

Approximately thirty of the women who made the bicentennial quilt became the nucleus for Wiltwyck, the largest quilter's guild in the Catskills. Formed in 1978, Wiltwyck at one time grew to 180 members, most of them women with little or no experience in quiltmaking to begin with. They came to learn. And behind all of this activity was Ruth Culver's guiding hand.

Her influence has been felt on a national level as well. Not only has Ruth taught individuals and groups as far away as Vermont, New Jersey, Pennsylvania and West Virginia, she has also been extremely active in the American Quilters Association. A dedicated teacher, Ruth helped form the program and the book for the National Quilters Association on "How to Teach Basic Quilt-making," because, as she states, "I was very determined that people were going to do it right." She is a certified judge of quilts, and she has advised the NQA on their certified appraisal program. The experience she garnered from the bicentennial quilt and from the biennial quilt shows put on by Wiltwyck came together in a book Ruth authored which shares her knowledge of how to plan, organize and hold a quilt show.

During the course of twenty very active years of promoting the art of quiltmaking and teaching others, Ruth somehow found the time to make quilts and wall-hangings for her home, her children and her grandchildren. And she has sold a few items as well. There is always a work-in-progress and others that are planned. "You're usually planning another quilt as you're making one," Ruth explained. "You always have two or three others planned." As Ruth Culver has enriched the art of quiltmaking in the Catskills, so has quiltmaking enriched and rewarded her life: "Quilting is a giving thing—a giving of yourself and giving to each other. And sharing. It's a very caring kind of thing. I've never found anything else which quite fits the bill like quilting does." [Ruth Culver, 1993]

Marie Genthner (b. 1907)

PHOTOGRAPH 1985, COURTESY OF THE ERPF CATSKILL CULTURAL
CENTER'S FOLKLIFE PROGRAM.

At eighty-six years of age, her dexterity hindered by arthritis which has left her fingers without feeling, making it difficult to thread needles—or even to pick up a needle—Marie Genthner still keeps her sewing basket by her chair. As she recovers from a broken hip suffered in the summer of 1993, Marie is nearly confined to that chair, the monotony of the long days broken by plying the arts of piecework and applique she first learned in 1928. Fingers that used to fly through fabric now move much more haltingly, and the effort cannot be sustained for long. One's first impression might be, "Here is a person with cause for complaint." But Marie is singularly cheerful, her reminiscences punctuated with smiles and laughter. And she is still creating quilted art of great beauty.

Marie was born in 1907 in "that foreign country, Brooklyn," as she likes to say. Her father was an immigrant from Austria-Hungary who brought his apprenticed skills as a baker to the new world and immediately went into business for himself. Brooklyn, then as now, pulsed with life, the streets swarming with people; the little bakery thrived. Marie remembers how her father would go down to the Brooklyn docks and hire bakers straight off the boats from Europe, bringing the new employees home to live with the family in the rooms above the shop.

As the bakery grew and prospered, Marie's father, in search of a better life—the same impulse which drove him from Central Europe years before—set his sights on the Catskill Mountains. Fearing that the daily rigors of a Brooklyn bakery were too hard on his wife, he bought a rambling farmhouse in Lake Katrine, Ulster County, in 1920 and turned it into a summer boarding house. In those days, Marie notes, "everybody wanted to go to the country for two weeks." And "the country," to New Yorkers, meant the Catskills.

In an ironic foreshadowing of the present-day burst of bed and breakfast inns, which seem to crop up overnight like mushrooms after a summer rain—and disappear almost as quickly—Marie's family discovered the long hours and hard work of the hospitality industry. "That was harder than the bakery!" Marie laughs. "For one thing, you had to carry drinking water. Mother did all the cooking and we [the children] did all the pumping."

The family worked as a team from dawn to dusk to cater to their guests. One can only guess the impression made on vacationing New Yorkers by the absence of indoor plumbing. Perhaps they thought it quaint, or rustic. For Marie, however, the memory lingers of darting out at night to use the "outdoor facilities" facing ice and snow, sub-zero temperatures or driving rains, often with the irascible family rooster in hot pursuit.

So Marie's father went back into the bakery business. He turned the cellar of the boardinghouse into a bakery and drove his own truck around Lake Katrine selling his goods. After functioning as baker and distributor for a couple of years, he began to recognize the benefits of having a shop on a street in a town where customers came to *him*. The family moved, once again, to the village of Saugerties, where Marie still resides today.

For Marie, the move to Saugerties meant she no longer had to strap on snowshoes to traipse to the Lake Katrine depot for the train carrying her to school in Kingston. She also met the man who would soon become her husband. He was welcomed not only into the family, but into the family business. "My father said, 'If you're gonna hang around here, you gotta learn to be a baker,'" Marie recalls. Learn it he did. Marie and her husband worked in her father's bakery until her father retired. Then they took it over and operated it themselves for the next forty-three years.

It was a busy family into which Marie was born. Her mother had little time for artistic pursuits, but she taught Marie the only craft she knew—crochet. It wasn't until she met her husband's family that Marie was introduced to the arts of patchwork and quiltmaking. Her mother-in-law and all three sisters-in-law "did patchwork," Marie states. "They quilted some, but mostly patchwork. 'Course, you could have a quilt quilted by ladies who just did the quilting."

Marie began her first quilt in 1927 while she was pregnant with her first child. She would piece a top together and then take it to the Ladies Aid Society of the nearby Reformed Church in High Woods. They would add the batting and the backing and quilt the layers together. "They would charge by the number of spools of thread that they would use," Marie says. "It was, like, a dollar and a quarter per spool ... and you never paid more than ten dollars to have a quilt quilted. Never."

Marie had a penchant for crib quilts, which she would complete entirely on her own, but she would not quilt them—she would tie them off, or "knot them" as she prefers to say. Aside from the crib quilts she would design and execute on her own, Marie and her in-laws spent many hours together making crib quilts from old unfinished tops left behind by her husband's grandmother.

From the moment Marie first learned to piece a quilt top, quilt-making became part of her daily routine, her sewing basket her constant companion. She would steal a few quiet minutes between customers at the bakery to work on a square, or relax with some piece-work in the evenings in the apartment above the store after the children were asleep. For the next sixty-six years, much of Marie's spare time was devoted to quiltmaking.

Though she steadily refined her piecing and applique techniques, it was not until the mid-1970s that Marie began to quilt her own tops instead of paying to have them quilted. She met Ruth Culver and participated in the Ulster County bicentennial quilt, contributing one of the pictorial blocks and then helping with the quilting.

That experience inspired her to coordinate the making of a bicentennial quilt for her home village of Saugerties. Marie networked through her friends and bakery customers and proudly notes that over seventy people eventually became involved in the project, a community-wide endeavor. Twenty years later, sadly enough, the result of that tremendous outpouring of community pride and industry suffers from unfortunate neglect. "We never did find a place to hang it," Marie says. "It's just in somebody's house."

After the bicentennial year had passed, Marie, like many women throughout the Catskills, missed the camaraderie of working with others on joint projects. She joined the newly-formed Wiltwyck guild in Kingston, and a few years later she became one of the founding members of the South Mountain Piecemakers, a smaller guild in Saugerties. Retired by this point, Marie began to teach classes in "lap quilting" ("quilt-as-you-go") in her apartment above the bakery because, she says, "When we closed up finally, I missed the people so much, you know?" One of her students was her own daughter, who has become a very accomplished quiltmaker in her own right.

Marie has made forty-four quilts to date, plus many wall-hangings. They are all hand-pieced or hand-appliqued, and since the mid-1970s, all hand-quilted personally by Marie. Many feature a central medallion of appliqued floral motifs expressing Marie's love of gardening.

Since her retirement, however, quiltmaking has had to compete for Marie's time with a more recently-acquired talent, weaving, taught and inspired by Berta Frye of Bearsville who taught herself the art during the course of volunteer hospital work during World War II. Berta and her sister would visit wounded servicemen in area hospitals, distracting them from their injuries by reading or talking to them or engaging them in a game of checkers. One day a wounded soldier told Berta that he would like to learn weaving. Berta went to the library, found a book on weaving and applied herself to mastering the difficult craft so she could teach the soldier. "It was a privilege to know her," Marie says, a sentiment anyone who has met Marie Genthner could just as assuredly apply to her.

Mary Lowe (b. 1947)

Mary Lowe, in a Paris studio, 1995. The 32" by 35" wall-hanging, titled "Contradiction," was machine- and hand-pieced, and hand-quilted by Mary in 1991. Mary wrote: "This was created as a result of a challenge in a small quilt group, 'The Seven Sisters,' in Brampton, Ontario. The challenge was to use a diamond shape within your piece ... When this quilt is viewed, you sometimes see baby blocks or eight pointed stars or chevrons or just interesting colors. I did most of the hand piecing in the car on the way to Quilt Canada in Ottawa (a national quilting conference)."

*M*ary Lowe, like many of the post-WWII "baby-boomer" generation, has led a highly mobile, almost nomadic life. She spent but a brief eight years in the Catskills, but she left an indelible mark on the region's quiltmaking, as she has done wherever her travels take her. Like a Johnny Appleseed of quiltmaking, art blooms along the trail she leaves behind.

Mary's journey began in 1947 in Williamsville, New York (near Buffalo). From the very beginning, quilts were a part of her life. "I never knew my great-grandmother," Mary says, "but I know her work well. She made some beautiful quilts. As a child growing up ... I always slept under one of her quilts." Many of those quilts were pieced "scrap quilts." "I loved looking at the different fabrics," Mary recalls. The artful juxtaposition of multiple colors and shades of various fabrics was to remain a lifelong fascination for Mary.

By 1974, Mary was married and living in Souderton, Pennsylvania. Her neighbor was a Mennonite and retired nurse who supplemented her pension by quilting for other people. "She always had two or three quilts on frames and would have quilting bees several times a week," Mary recalls. "She would show me all the new quilt tops and the quilts when they were finished."

When Mary's sister-in-law was expecting her first child, Mary decided to make a quilt for the baby with her neighbor's help. But the neighbor only quilted; she didn't make tops. Mary was on her own. "I went to the local five and dime and bought animal squares to embroider," she says. "When they were completed, I appliqued them to a yellow muslin sheet. Can you imagine?" she adds, somewhat ruefully. The top completed, her neighbor then showed her how to mark the top, baste the layers together and quilt along the marked pattern. Maybe not a "Best of Show" quilt when it was completed, but even so, Mary states, "Boy, was I proud of that quilt."

In 1976 Mary was off to Connecticut for three years, then another three years were spent in Boise, Idaho. She continued to make quilts on her own, learning new patterns from the few books and magazines available at that time. She tried many of the classic patterns, like "Sunbonnet Sue" and "Dresden Plate," and, while in Idaho, she made her first "scrap quilt" in emulation of her great-grandmother's work. She taught herself the counted cross-stitch embroidery technique and incorporated it into her quiltmaking. But aside from her Mennonite friend's instruction, Mary, up to that point, had never taken a class or joined a guild. "As a matter of fact," she says, "I didn't know they even existed."

All that changed when Mary and her family moved to Saugerties, Ulster County, in 1982. When she heard about the Wiltwyck Guild in neighboring Kingston, she immediately joined, signing up for workshops within the guild and enrolling in Ruth Culver's quiltmaking course at Ulster County Community College. After eight years of working on her own, learning by trial and error, the formal instruction was welcome. "It's amazing how much I didn't know, and how much easier everything became," Mary recalls.

Mary's years in Ulster County–1982 to 1990–transformed her quiltmaking hobby into a consuming avocation and mature art form. Her talent and enthusiasm convinced Ruth Culver that Mary should become a teacher herself. Thus encouraged, Mary taught her first class in basic quiltmaking at a local fabric store in 1985. Soon, teaching became a new passion for Mary. That first class led to many more, in many different locations, including taking over Ruth Culver's quiltmaking course at UCCC when Ruth decided to stop teaching there. Mary proudly points out that many of her former students later became active members of Wiltwyck.

And Mary herself became increasingly more active in Wiltwyck; she served on the board, and she was elected president of the guild her final year in New York. She also started a separate quiltmaking chapter, the South Mountain Piecemakers, in her home town of Saugerties. In addition to refining her talents and imbuing her with true dedication to the art of quiltmaking, Mary's sojourn in the Catskills, and her association with the quilters she met here, instilled in her a sense of community involvement and service which she carried with her on her subsequent travels.

In 1990, the Lowe family hit the road again, this time to Canada. Mary immediately joined two quiltmaking guilds in Toronto, becoming especially active in one by teaching, serving on the board and starting "a few new committees, which I chaired," she states. One of those committees, "Community Projects," carried to Canada the American quilt guild principle of community service. Under Mary's direction, the guild made four quilts each year for charity, as well as quilted placemats for the "Meals on Wheels" program, and baby quilts for the Sick Children's Hospital. She also assisted one other guild and two other community organizations in the making of raffle quilts.

Newly arrived in Tucson, Arizona, in 1993, Mary writes, "I am still quilting, but am not involved in the local guild (yet)." She is a full-time student studying sign language interpreting, and she performs volunteer work at the Arizona State School for the Deaf and Blind where she has been asked to institute a program teaching quiltmaking. "I can't wait to start," Mary writes. "My biggest reward is seeing the progress of students."

Mary's own quiltmaking is a continual tug-of-war between tradition and experimentation. She likes to learn new techniques, like natural dyeing; "It is fun, but it can be hard for me to break away from the totally traditional quilts," she writes. "I prefer traditional quilting and quilts, but need to stretch myself at times. I don't want to get stagnant."

Mary loves to make old-fashioned "charm" quilts and "scrap" quilts because, "They remind me of my childhood," she says. The quilts she has been commissioned to make, or has made as class samples, "have been traditional methods and patterns," she adds, although she drafts the design for those traditional patterns on her computer.

The quilts Mary makes for herself express her more experimental side. They resemble abstract painting: "When I am making a quilt for myself for pure pleasure, I like to play around with color," she writes. "I have enjoyed doing color washes using 2 1/2 inch squares of hundreds of fabrics. First I choose a picture of a painting or a photo, and then pull fabrics of the same colors that are in that picture. I do not try to reproduce the picture, just play with the colors to create pleasing movement and shadowing."

Her technique exhibits the same blend of the modern and the traditional. She teaches "quick piecing" as well as traditional piecing, and depending upon the purpose for which the quilt is destined, sometimes she hand-pieces and sometimes she pieces on her sewing machine. But, "I usually only hand-quilt," she writes. "Occasionally I will machine quilt a piece, but again it depends on whether it is to be an heirloom or a user."

Mary Lowe was a quiltmaker before she came to the Catskills, but it was while she was living in Ulster County, in the shade of the "Blue Mountains" along the Hudson River, that Mary Lowe became an artist in cloth. She left a part of herself behind when she moved away, but she also took a small piece of the Catskills away with her:

> When I do my color washes or my natural dyeing, the colors that I gravitate to are the colors that you see in the Catskill Mountains—especially the fall colors ... Even though I was not raised in the Catskills, I felt more at home there than anywhere else I have lived. As you know, I have lived in several different areas of the country as well as Canada, and have quilted in many of them. I found the interest to be the greatest in the Catskills. People were eager to learn and unafraid to try new methods. Most of the quilters I knew were not trying to make statements, they were making heirlooms—nice warm loving quilts. [Mary Lowe, 1993]

Katherine Mouser (b. 1942)

THE 38" BY 38" WALL-HANGING, "SAN MARCO DI VENEZIA," WAS HAND-
PIECED AND HAND-QUILTED BY KATHERINE, COMPLETED IN 1991. THE CEN-
TER IS A REPRODUCTION OF A SECTION OF THE MARBLE FLOOR OF ST.
MARK'S CATHEDRAL IN VENICE, AND THE BACKGROUND IS THE "KANSAS
DUGOUT" PATTERN. KATHERINE WROTE: "WHEN I DRAFTED THE CURVED
PIECE, I COULDN'T IMAGINE THAT A STONECUTTER COULD CUT SUCH A
POINT, BUT WHEN I FINALLY SAW A COMMERCIAL POSTCARD OF THE FLOOR,
THAT'S EXACTLY THE SHAPE OF THE PIECE."

Katherine Mouser no longer uses a quilting frame or hoop; it restricts her freedom of movement. When a quilt top is finished, she assembles the three layers and bastes it very closely to hold it together so she can quilt on her lap wherever she goes. "The quilt I made my first grandchild," she says, by way of illustration, "I quilted in three or four different airports, in four or five different states. I took it to the child's great-grandfather's funeral to quilt." Then she quickly corrects herself, "I mean the trip to the funeral."

Travel is nothing new to Katherine because her father was in the FBI. As a child and teenager, Katherine found herself moving from city to city across the country because her father was periodically reassigned.

She was born in 1942 in Los Angeles, where she spent her first early years. "In California," Katherine recalls, "quilts were not the utilitarian bedcovers that they were in the East. The weather was not conducive to quilts. And the only family quilts that we have—and we do have some—are very, very thin and delicate." They were "scrap quilts" pieced in traditional patterns, such as "Bow Tie," and they were made by one of Katherine's grandmothers, who died when Katherine was three years old. Because they are so thin, the quilting is very close and fine but, unfortunately, Katherine never had the opportunity to see the work as it was being done.

"I was not aware of quilts at all until I was probably twelve years old," Katherine continues. By then, the family was living in Kansas City, the nineteenth-century gateway to the west. Katherine developed an interest in quilts as an outgrowth of a new-found fascination with the westward movement and the women who once ventured forth from Kansas City carrying their heirloom quilts in covered wagons.

But that early interest in quilts gradually receded and then disappeared, not to reawaken again for another twenty years. Katherine's mother "insisted I learn to sew," Katherine recalls, "and I hated sewing. I was not a very cooperative child." Her mother, a career librarian, "sewed a great deal," Katherine continued. "She made clothes and curtains and bedspreads, but not quilts. She didn't believe in wasting time like that."

Katherine became a proficient needle-worker in spite of being "uncooperative." Later, as a young mother, she made clothes for herself and her daughter and she enjoyed making them because, as she explained, "nobody was standing there telling me I had to do it." The need for a more creative outlet also began to manifest itself around that same time. Her husband was in the navy, and Katherine began to study oil painting to fill her time while he was at sea. They were living in Virginia, a state with a rich quiltmaking tradition, but "I was a navy wife in a big city," Katherine said. "I really didn't get interested in quilts until I came up here [to the Catskills]."

Katherine and her family moved in 1970 to Lake Katrine, Ulster County, a rural community between the village of Saugerties and the city of Kingston. A teacher by profession, Katherine found that she was not certified to teach in the state of New York. She now had two children to raise and did not have the time, nor the inclination, to take the requisite courses, so she began to cast about for an alternate use of her time. In 1975, "I saw an ad in a newspaper that said they were going to teach quilting classes in the Kingston Plaza in a community room," Katherine said. The teacher was Ruth Culver, who has inspired and encouraged many budding quiltmakers in the Catskills. Katherine attended that first class and a new passion was born: "The bug bit, and bit hard," she says.

It was the year before the bicentennial, the birth date of the modern era in quiltmaking, and "there were not many books out," Katherine recalls. "There were not patterns out. And that was what was fun, because I like to make up my own, draft my own. That was exciting. It was kind of 'find your own way.' And we ate up every book that came out anyway. It was consuming, but I was ready to be consumed." For a few years thereafter, "I did nothing but quilt," Katherine adds.

Quiltmaking not only satisfied her artistic inclinations, it allowed her to indulge her passion for teaching. Shortly after that first class at the Kingston Plaza, Katherine became a quiltmaking instructor herself. By 1993, she estimated that she had taught "several hundred" students at libraries, quilt stores, guild meetings, quilt shows and Ulster County Community College adult education courses. "I was supporting my habit by teaching," Katherine says. With the money earned, "I could buy more fabric," she adds, a trend she sees as common among quiltmakers. "There is this need to have fabric, even though you're not sure what you're going to do with it. We all have this stash. And now the challenge is to make something without buying anything."

In eighteen years, Katherine produced 40-50 works of quilted art, some of which she sold. "If you want to make $1.25 an hour, make quilts," she advises. She prefers pieced designs, such as stars and traditional patterns like "Jacob's Ladder" and "Kansas Dugout," because "I like geometrics," she says. "I love working with grids, love working with compasses."

Her favorite project was a quilt in which she tried to replicate the pattern of the marble floor of Saint Mark's Cathedral in Venice. It all started when her son showed her a black and white photo he had taken, exclaiming, "There's this quilt stuff all over the floor!" Intrigued, Katherine began to plot the design on graph paper, color it in, and then translate it into cloth. "I had to guess at the colors," she says, and as it turns out, "they're all wrong. Several people have sent me pictures of it. The colors are supposed to be browns and oranges, and I did it in pinks and tans."

Chromatically accurate or not, the quilt is an artistic success in every regard. Remembering the design difficulties, Katherine comments, "It was quite a feat to draft because it looked as if pieces were cut very strangely from the marble [segments comprising a circle came to a long tapering point]. I thought, 'Nobody would cut a piece of marble like that!' But I did it that way anyway, and the pictures show that's the way they were cut."

That project, and subsequent experience, has brought home to Katherine the universality of human experience. "Many of the patterns on that floor are recognizable American quilt patterns," she says. "Now, that was done in the fifteenth and fourteenth century. It shows to me that, if you give a person a grid and a pencil, they're going to come up with some of the same designs. There are just so many ways you can put something together. We sit down and we think we've invented something, and it turns out that it's been around. Recently, I was in Egypt with my mother and we looked at mosaics that were recognizable things that we use as quilt patterns. We're all made of the same stuff, and we create the same stuff."

No artist, however, can truly be content with the idea that there is nothing new under the sun. Katherine is no exception, for she quickly adds, "But as you look at them, quilts all seem to be different. And they all speak of the person who made them."

The bug is not biting as hard as it once did. "It will always be a passion," Katherine says, but "it's no longer the driving force in my life. I've made my last king-size quilt, I think." She was one of the charter members of Wiltwyck, and served a term as president, but she admits that she isn't very active in guild work any more. However, "I still have a lot of quilts in my head that are undone," she adds.

The Greeks invented the Muses to try to explain and understand artistic inspiration. Katherine ended her interview with an eloquent summation of the artist's sense of wonder when standing face to face with her own best creation:

> *The one I made for my son* [from the photograph of the floor of Saint Mark's Cathedral]*—I just thought I would never get it done. I always see it twice a year when I go out to visit it—excuse me, to visit him.* [she laughed] *Freudian! I'll say, 'I can't really believe I did that.' There is a detachment from personal responsibility. In the end, when the whole thing is finished, there's almost this metaphysical question, 'Did I really make that?' The answer is 'Well, not quite.' Because it suddenly has taken on its own personality, and I don't feel responsible for it.* [Katherine Mouser, 1994]

Evelyn Nabors (b. 1914)

THE WALL-HANGING, "TRIANGLES," WAS PIECED AND HAND-QUILTED BY EVELYN, USING TRIANGULAR PIECES LEFT OVER FROM A LARGE QUILT. THE PATTERN IS A REPRODUCTION FROM AN ANTIQUE QUILT EVELYN ONCE SAW.

*Q*uiltmaking calls for a certain intrepidity of spirit, each stitch among the thousands required for a full-size quilt being but one small step in the journey toward completion. As in any art, one must remain undaunted by the intense competition, the brilliant work one sees at every quilt show. One's artistic soul must be ready to make that leap of faith required to plot, plan and execute a new original within a time-honored and centuries-old art form. For Evelyn Nabors, that restless and eager spirit is not content to stay channeled in quiltmaking. New avenues of expression are constantly sought. "Do I get involved in anything and everything? I do," Evelyn says.

Several of the quiltmakers interviewed for this book who find themselves in circumstances similar to Evelyn's—retired, widowed, living alone—stated that they quilted to "pass the time" or "to keep busy." With Evelyn Nabors, it is just the opposite. Her skills and interests are so far-ranging that she has to budget her time to try to fit everything in. "I'm divided now because I want to quilt, but I also want to weave," she says, proudly displaying the large loom next to her quilting frame in her living room. Her interest in fabric creation has even gone the next step further; she has recently taken up spinning. One would not be surprised to soon find sheep grazing in her yard, or a stand of cotton growing in her field. Cheerfully approaching eighty years of age, Evelyn is still branching out into new endeavors, most of which slow down in the warmer months because, as she explains, "beginning in May, the golf season starts."

Evelyn Nabors is a relative newcomer to the Catskills. She was born in 1914 in the Woodhaven section of Queens and lived most of her life in or around New York City, aside from a tour of duty in Hawaii as a WAVE during World War II. Consistent with the experience of many women of her generation, sewing was a part of Evelyn's early education. Evelyn's mother made clothes for the family—dresses and coats—although "of course, when you're a child you like the store-bought kind better," Evelyn admitted. "As a child I made doll's clothes," she continued. "I don't think the kids do that anymore." And Evelyn was introduced to quiltmaking by her aunt, who was active in a church society on Long Island. They made mostly aprons and other smaller—and faster to pro-duce—craft items, but occasionally they would make a quilt, and when they did, Evelyn would help her aunt by cutting out the pieces for the top.

After Evelyn graduated from high school, she attended the Pratt Institute for one year to study dressmaking, but the life of a professional seamstress was not for her. "It's all right to sew for yourself," she stated. "If you blow it, it's okay. But to make something for somebody else .... " So Evelyn chose office work instead, reserving her sewing skills for her own use, making her own clothes and producing her first quilts at home in the evenings. Those early quilts were a far cry from the full-size, hand-quilted, hand-appliqued works she would produce in later years. Evelyn explained, "My friends would have a baby, and I would make a baby quilt. Years ago you used to be able to buy a kit. Some of them were stamped with a pattern for a baby quilt." In spite of the fact that all of those early baby quilts were tied, and many of them came from kits, the final products became instant heirlooms. As Evelyn recalled, "A number of the people that I gave quilts to years ago were telling me that they kept them for their kids when they grew up."

As life became busier with marriage, family and career, Evelyn had less time for quiltmaking, but she never gave it up entirely. Even when she was in the navy during World War II she found spare moments to work on one quilt top, a special going-away present from friends back home in New York. "I saw it in Gimbels," she said. "A quilt top with appliques." Similar to the baby quilts she had made previously, "the material came in a kit, and the top was stamped. The appliques you cut out and then appliqued on." Evelyn still has that quilt today, carefully appliqued and tied together fifty years ago in the middle of the Pacific war.

Her interest in quiltmaking quickened in the mid-1950s when she hand-pieced a top for a full-size quilt as a gift for some friends of hers. Church societies began to give her the scraps saved from making aprons and other items, and Evelyn began to haunt dry goods stores. "I remember going to a store and buying a quarter of a yard of this, a quarter of a yard of that. You don't see that kind of store any more," Evelyn says. But Evelyn still did not do any actual quilting. She would tie the layers together, or send the top to a church society and pay them to quilt it for her.

It wasn't until Evelyn and her husband retired and moved to New Paltz in 1969 that she began to hand-quilt her tops, and in the process she became one of the most active members of the quilting revival in Ulster County. The catalyst for Evelyn, as it was for hundreds of women in the Catskills, was the 1976 bicentennial. She made a square for the New Paltz bicentennial quilt, and then helped to quilt it at the town library. It was not only her first experience in hand-quilting, but her first involvement in working together with other quilters on a communal project. That quilt was followed two years later by another group quilt for the tricentennial celebration of the founding of the village of New Paltz. Those experiences helped Evelyn integrate into her new community. "That was when I really got to know people," she confides. "Quilting has helped me so much."

A core group of six women who worked on the tricentennial quilt decided to continue to meet and quilt together after that project was finished. They began to gather at Evelyn's home every Wednesday from October to May. Evelyn took a course in "Intermediate Quilting" under the instruction of Ruth Culver at Ulster County Community College, and she joined Wiltwyck soon thereafter. Her energy and knowledge placed her in the role of leader and teacher for her Wednesday group. "What I learned at guild, I brought back here," she states. She also began to teach a quilting class in the New Paltz Reformed Church, and when Mary Lowe started the South Mountain Piecemakers guild in Saugerties in 1982, Evelyn joined there as well.

With all of these meetings, workshops and classes to attend–and learning to weave and spin in her "spare time"–Evelyn still somehow found the time to make over twenty full-size quilts and dozens of baby quilts. And a busy schedule does not mean the quality of the work must suffer. Only once did Evelyn decide that she would sell one of her quilts. It was a striking floral applique which had won "Best of Show" at Wiltwyck. Evelyn, with the attitude, as she said, of "If they want it, they got it," put a price of $2000 on that quilt. It sold immediately. And she has also exhibited her quilts at the prestigious Auburn Art Museum. "They take everyone from all over the world," Evelyn explained. "They only accept about 130 pieces. To get a prize? No way. I'm only a beginner or intermediate compared to what comes in. Everything's relative. In that kind of a field, you're not advanced.

You're against professionals and really beautiful work. So if I can get accepted, that's the honor."

As the 1993 golf season draws to a close, Evelyn Nabors will begin to devote more of her time to weaving, spinning and quilting, juggling those interests to find time to devote to each. Her Wednesday morning group will begin to gather again in her living room each week, Wiltwyck will resume its monthly meetings and the South Mountain Piecemakers will begin to work on their next raffle quilt. And Evelyn Nabors, as she approaches her eightieth year, will circulate through all of this activity learning new skills, and teaching and inspiring others. "I don't get bored," she says, with characteristic understatement.

Hilda Pleva (b. 1945)

PHOTOGRAPH, 1985. COURTESY OF THE ERPF CATSKILL CULTURAL CENTER'S FOLKLIFE PROGRAM.

"*E*very organization which has been primarily female has undergone a lot of change within the last twenty to twenty-five years," states Hilda Pleva. And Hilda sees her own life as a paradigm of that change. She was very active in quiltmaking and guild organization in the late 1970s and early 1980s when her children were young and she was happily married, but since her separation from her husband in 1983 Hilda has had no time for guild work and precious little time to devote to her own quilt projects. On those rare occasions when Hilda does have the chance to attend a meeting of Wiltwyck, she now sees mostly younger women with little children, or older women whose children have grown. "The changes that we have seen in society are reflected in all of these groups," says Hilda. "We have many, many more women who are working full-time." And those women, like Hilda herself, cannot spare the hundreds of hours needed for quiltmaking.

Hilda Pleva did not begin making quilts until 1974 when she moved from Connecticut to Kingston, but as a child she was surrounded by female relatives skilled in dressmaking, embroidery, knitting, crocheting–every sewing skill, in fact, except quiltmaking. She was born in New York City in 1945 while her father was stationed with the air force in Guam, "which makes me one of the first baby-boomers," she says. She grew up in the Bensonhurst section of Brooklyn, and it was there that she first learned handcrafts, learning to knit and crochet by the age of ten. The Catskills were a far-off wonderland she would visit for a couple of weeks each summer, staying with a German family in Coxsackie, "picking berries and vegetables in a garden and herding turkeys," she recalls; "Certainly things I didn't get a chance to do in Brooklyn."

When she married and moved to Connecticut, Hilda began to see more quilts, but she still had never met anyone who made quilts. Those were the fallow years for quiltmaking, the 1960s and early 1970s, when quiltmaking seemed to be a dead archaic art. The pivotal moment for Hilda arrived when she met Ruth Culver the summer she moved to Kingston and, "eager to get into the community and meet people," she enrolled that fall in Ruth's quiltmaking class at Ulster County Community College. Hilda immediately "loved the geometrics of it and loved the color," but, she adds, "I was very disappointed the first time I sat at a quilting frame and had to do those tiny little stitches with a thimble." The quilting stitch is hard work, and it takes time and patience to achieve proficiency. But through her perseverance, "It turns out that the aspect of quilting I enjoy the most is the hand-quilting," Hilda states.

Hilda soon became one of the key figures in the quiltmaking revival in Kingston. Along with forty-one other women from Ruth Culver's classes, she worked on the Ulster County bicentennial quilt, and afterwards she became a charter member of Wiltwyck, eventually serving a two-year term as president. She joined the National Quilters Association and became certified by that organization as a teacher of "Beginning Quilting." She taught workshops within Wiltwyck, held classes in her home and in area fabric stores, and she demonstrated quilting at the Ulster County Quilt Exposition. A born teacher, Hilda developed her own program to introduce school children to quiltmaking. She traveled from school to school, visiting different classrooms to make her presentation while dressed in colonial costume. Few individuals have devoted themselves as thoroughly and as selflessly to promoting the art of quiltmaking as Hilda Pleva did between 1975 and 1984. And all the while she was raising three young children.

Those activities came to an abrupt halt in 1983 when Hilda Pleva and her husband separated. She was now on her own with the three children, and she had to return to work as an elementary school teacher. Not a person to be broken by adversity, Hilda started taking classes at night and by 1988 she had earned her second master's degree, this time in library science. Soon after, she acquired a position as a school librarian. Hilda used to produce a full-size hand-quilted quilt in six months. As of the summer of 1993, she had not completed a quilt since 1984.

But her interest in quiltmaking has not waned. She has a few works-in-progress that she turns to in her few hours of spare time. "I have found," she says, "that it's very important for me, for my mental health, to allow myself time for some creative expression, and quilting remains very important to me—the feeling of making something that no one else has made, of doing something very unique." Her love of hand-quilting has led her to concentrate on making wholecloth quilts and quilts using the Amish style of solid colors because "the hand-quilting really shows up best on solids," she says. She has also found the time to make some quilted wall-hangings and has dabbled in pillows and machine-applique, works that Hilda refers to as "peripheral arts."

Hilda still reads extensively about quiltmaking, picking up every new book and magazine on the subject, and she calls herself a "fabric-holic," always collecting material. She regrets that she used to sell her work in the days when she was producing quilted art at a steady pace: "It's a little painful to go into other people's homes and see your best work on their wall," she says. But if the fates are kind and there are no future disruptions in Hilda Pleva's life, her opinions on quiltmaking in general leave no doubt that she will make many more quilts to replace those, when time and circumstances allow: "I feel it's always been an art. There are artsy-craftsy things that come into vogue and go out of vogue. They're not traditional, and they just come and go. Quilting is traditional, and it's never going to be out of style. It has a rooted place." From Bensonhurst to Connecticut to Kingston ... one hopes that Hilda's own roots in the Catskills have grown and spread to the extent that she will not be tempted to move on when the children are grown or when she finally retires from the schools and libraries. Hers is a voice that is strong, clear, committed, intelligent and articulate. If the Catskills are to earn acknowledgment of its rightful place as a worldwide center for the art of quiltmaking, it needs women such as Hilda to speak for it. And she knows the value of art—her art, and the art of others:

> My mother now, who is approaching seventy and still paints—I keep telling her, 'Will you clean less and paint more while you still can!' Because her clean floors will disappear, but her paintings will never disappear. And that's part of this, too. It's our reach for immortality, to leave something behind. [Hilda Pleva, 1993]

Nancy Smith (b. 1937)

PHOTOGRAPH COLLECTION OF THE CATSKILL MOUNTAIN QUILTERS HALL OF FAME.

𝒯he recent history of quiltmaking in the Catskill Mountains would tell an entirely different story were it not for Nancy Smith. She was the founder, not only of the Catskill Mountain Quilters Hall of Fame, but of one of the region's most talented and traditional guilds as well. Her relocation to Kingston in 1992, moving from her ancestral home high in the central Catskills, placed her in temporary retirement from active roles in quiltmaking organizations, but she will never give up the art of quiltmaking itself. "It's therapy, and it's addictive," she said. "And once you start you just always quilt, I guess ... If you're a quilter, you're a quilter. I don't know of anybody that's given it up."

Nancy says the word "quilter" with respect, almost reverence. During a discussion about the recent importation of inexpensive quilts from China, Nancy stated, "They look nice ... If you're not a quilter, you wouldn't see a difference between one that I did and one that they did. [But] a quilter would know the difference." In Nancy Smith's vocabulary, the word "quilter" denotes knowledge, expertise and dedication. She worked side-by-side with some of the finest of the older generation of Catskill Mountains quiltmakers. Consequently, she is a staunch traditionalist and purist. To be conferred the title "quilt," the work must be hand-quilted, not tied-off or machine-quilted. Nothing less will do. As Nancy said, "If you spend three hundred hours [hand-] quilting a quilt, you know what a quilt is."

Nancy Smith was born in 1937 in the village of Pine Hill in northern Ulster County. Her ancestors first came to the Catskills five generations before her, and their careers read like an index to the region. They were involved "in everything–quarries, tanning, merchants, tourist trade, farmers," Nancy stated, "but none of them quilters, that I know of." She continued, "I really don't know how I got into it. As far as I know, my mother couldn't even sew on a button." The only sewing Nancy recalls doing as a child was making "yo-yo's"–a fad once popular for bedspreads, made from fabric remnants and employing techniques similar to those used in piecing a quilt top.

When she was a teenager, however, she joined the Ladies Aid Society of the Pine Hill Methodist Church, which held quilting bees. Members of the community would donate quilt tops to the Society, which would then quilt them and raffle them off, or sell them at their bazaar. The quilts would usually sell for between 50 and 75 dollars–a goodly sum in the early 1950s.

The Society eventually disbanded, and for almost twenty years Nancy gave little thought to quiltmaking. Then the arts and crafts boom of the early 1970s gave rise to numerous cottage industries in the Catskills, and Nancy was hired by one in nearby Oliverea called Puckihuddle, which specialized in hand-sewn products, including quilts. "They had a lot of people in the area sewing for them," Nancy recalled.

A few years later, when Puckihuddle folded, Nancy and her sister-in-law began to quilt tops for other people, and eventually she opened her own store. But something was missing. As Nancy explained, "I just felt quilting was kind of a social thing. They'd always had quilting bees. You get to the point where you just want to talk about things like that to other people who know what you're talking about." So she put an ad in *The Catskill Mountain News* in 1979 advertising the formation of a quilting guild, and the women who responded became the Catskill Mountain Quilters Guild. They have been meeting once a week ever since.

The talent that came out of the surrounding hills and hamlets and gathered in Nancy Smith's husband's gun shop for their weekly quilting bees so impressed Nancy that she began to formulate the idea for the Catskill Mountain Quilters Hall of Fame. She was not the only one so impressed. When the guild became too large to continue to meet in the gun shop, they were invited to use the facilities of the Erpf Catskill Cultural Center in Arkville, which offered them the free use of one of its gallery rooms, complete with a large quilt frame suspended from the ceiling by pulleys. "Oh, a lot of them are gone now," Nancy said in 1993, but she still has a friendship quilt which was made for her by the original members of the guild. Each member made a block and embroidered her signature, and then the guild joined the blocks together and quilted it. More than a keepsake, it is an heirloom—as a quilt should be.

The Catskill Mountain Quilters Guild still meets every Monday in Arkville. They still feature wonderful talent and enthusiasm, but the organization that Nancy Smith set in motion back in 1979 now functions without her. Nancy Smith's life changed and she had to move on. She and a partner operated a crafts store in Kingston, and Nancy also worked full-time in a bank. Her daily schedule was full.

Nancy Smith's Wall Street crafts store featured Catskill Mountains handmade quilts offered for sale on consignment, but business was not good. "I think it's in another slump right now," she said. "From being in the shop and selling, fabric items are not moving, including the quilts. And we've got a couple of beauties. And people are just not buying them." Why? "You just can't beat China for prices," Nancy said. "So if somebody's gonna buy a quilt, they're gonna buy the $150 [Chinese] quilt over the $600 [American] quilt."

American quiltmaking–perhaps the most distinctively American art–never before as popular, innovative, widespread and flourishing as it has been in the 1970s, 1980s and early 1990s, is in danger of again undergoing a decline because of that other distinctly American institution, free enterprise. Inexpensive foreign-made quilts are strangling American quiltmakers. Many of the finest quiltmakers in the Catskills refuse to compete. They are proud, and they are very independent– another national trait. As Nancy Smith stated, "I don't quilt to sell anymore because you can't get your money back ... So any quilts I make now, I've given to my kids."

Because it is an art and a passion, Catskill Mountains quiltmakers will continue to produce great works, but their products will appear for sale in fewer numbers and with less frequency if this trend continues. Why should quilts be worth $400-$600, or more? Nancy Smith displayed her latest creation, a "'white on white' that I've been working on for three years for my daughter," she said.

Three years. And it is an exquisite work of art.

Amelia White (b. 1899)

PHOTOGRAPH CIRCA 1982. COLLECTION OF THE CATSKILL MOUNTAIN QUILTERS HALL OF FAME.

The day before she died in 1983, Amelia White presented what was to be her last quilt to one of her nieces, the last member of her family who had requested a quilt but had not yet received one from her. Amelia had labored lovingly on that quilt, sewing many thousands of tiny stitches by hand, even though she had suffered a partially-debilitating stroke almost three years prior. It marked the end of a long life that had been devoted in large measure to giving and sharing, and the outward expression of that caring nature, the gift shared, was more often than not a quilt.

Born in 1899 in Dry Brook, a small farming community in the western Catskills, Amelia could remember well a rural America which has since vanished. Included among her recollections were memories of walking barefoot in the summer months three miles to attend school or church.

In the early years of the twentieth century it was still considered an elementary part of a young girl's education to acquire sewing skills, and in rural America, where self-sufficiency was still a necessity, those skills were especially valued. By the age of twelve, Amelia was ready to learn the finer points of quiltmaking. Under her mother's careful instruction, Amelia began to piece doll quilts from fabric remnants. Those were thrifty times, nothing useful was spared, and Amelia even remembered cutting up her mother's wedding dress for use in quiltmaking.

Once her skills had been tested and proven on the miniature quilts, Amelia was allowed to help piece quilt tops for the family's beds. They were utility quilts, made solely for use, and most of them were tied, not quilted. Amelia would continue to make these "everyday" quilts through her teen years and during the early years of her marriage.

While still a teenager in Dry Brook, Amelia began what was to become a lifelong pattern of contributing her needle skills in service to her church. She remembered with fondness those early-twentieth-century quilting bees at the little church in Dry Brook, recalling how the men of the congregation would then join the women for dinner in the evening. When she and her husband moved to the village of Shandaken, Ulster County, Amelia went immediately to work for her new church, helping the Ladies Society finish quilts and other hand-worked items for the annual bazaar. Each year she also raffled off one of her own quilts to benefit the church.

As the years progressed, Amelia made fewer utility quilts. Instead, her designs became more colorful and elaborate, and she had the leisure to quilt most of her tops. Amelia was a very traditional quilt-maker. Her favorite patterns were the time-honored "Nine-Patch" and the labor-intensive "Grandmother's Flower Garden." Every stitch was hand-sewn, and for materials Amelia favored fabric remnants left over from her own handmade clothes, or chosen perhaps from the treasure-trove of fabric stored in her garage—part of a continuous rummage sale she operated for the church. The colorful remnants of multitudes of fabric fit perfectly into the design scheme of the mosaic of a "Grandmother's Flower Garden" or the kaleidoscope of a "Nine-Patch."

It is not known with any accuracy how many quilts Amelia White made, but for seventy-two years quiltmaking was an everyday part of her life. She lived quietly, far from the world of fad and fashion, labor-iously but contentedly fashioning quilt after quilt throughout all of the long years of the mid-twentieth century, when quiltmaking was an almost forgotten art. She lived long enough to witness the rebirth of quiltmaking in the 1970s, when magazines devoted exclusively to the art proliferated, offering new and ever-more-varied patterns to replace the old classics that Amelia used to clip from the back sections of peri-odicals like *American Agriculture* magazine.

Quiltmaking would not be what it is today were it not for a few women like Amelia White; scattered across the country, they worked in near obscurity and anonymity, keeping the tradition alive and accessible to later generations. In recognition of her seventy-two con-secutive years of devotion to the art, Amelia White was inducted into the Catskill Mountain Quilters Hall of Fame in its inaugural year of 1982.

"INSPIRATION" BY PHYLLIS CAMERON. HAND-PIECED, HAND-APPLIQUED AND HAND-QUILTED BY PHYLLIS OVER A THREE-YEAR PERIOD, COMPLETED IN 1994. PHYLLIS WROTE: "THIS QUILT IS MADE FROM SMALL SCRAPS OF LATE 30S OR EARLY 40S FABRICS FROM MY MOTHER'S SCRAP BASKET. THE FABRICS WERE REJECTS GIVEN TO HER BY A RELATIVE WHO WORKED IN A CLOTH FAC-TORY IN NEW JERSEY. THE FLOWERS IN THE BASKETS IN THE MEDALLION ARE BRODERIE PERSE. EXCEPT FOR THE STARBURST EFFECT IN THE MEDALLION, THE REMAINDER OF THE QUILT IS CONSTRUCTED OF TWO-INCH SQUARES. IT HAS APPROXIMATELY 2600 PIECES."

CHAPTER 5

Sullivan County

*I*n common with Greene County (and several other New York State counties), Sullivan County was named after a hero of the Revolution–General John Sullivan, who, together with General James Clinton, waged a devastating campaign during the summer of 1779 against pro-British Iroquois settlements in western New York. Such actions would not be considered politically correct in the 1990s, but to the vulnerable white inhabitants of that time along the line of frontier in the Catskills–including today's Sullivan County–it was the stuff of which heroes are made.

Sullivan, though one county inland from the Hudson River, was settled early (the mid-1600s) by a scattering of European farmers and traders. They were lured, in part, by what is still Sullivan's most distinguishing characteristic–its many rivers and waterways which drain the southern tier of the Catskills. The most conspicuous is the Delaware River, forming Sullivan's southwestern border with Pennsylvania, but lesser streams and rivers abound, and the county is dotted with small lakes. The twentieth century placed even more of Sullivan underwater, including some of its best farmland and entire communities, with the construction of six reservoirs.

For generations, Sullivan County remained almost entirely composed of small farms. Then the railroad came through in the 1870s, and Sullivan was gradually transformed into "Catskill Land." Easy rail access from New York meant that Sullivan was the quickest and least expensive place to escape to from the city's summertime heat and haze. New Yorkers flocked in droves to the rolling hills and cool lakes of Sullivan County, and Sullivan soon eclipsed all other Catskill Mountains counties as a center for tourism.

At first, as in the more northern counties, farmers took in boarders and small hotels sprang up. Then entire bungalow communities were formed, and the small hotels became huge resorts with hundreds of rooms, lavish dining facilities, sports complexes and nightclubs ... The Concord, Kutsher's, Grossinger's—names familiar to any devotee of late-night television twenty years ago.

It was the Las Vegas of its day, without the gambling. Almost an entire generation of entertainers—particularly comedians—started their careers in the resorts of Sullivan. For Americans who came of age in the 1940s and 1950s, Sullivan County *was* the Catskills.

Some of those grand resorts have now closed their doors, not for the season, but for good. Vacationing in Sullivan has become passe. More exciting and exotic destinations beckon. Rail and automobile travel made the Sullivan resorts, and plane travel has unmade them. Those resorts that have survived have adapted to the times by building 36-hole golf courses and catering to the convention trade. But the era of families packing their bags to vacation in Sullivan for the summer is largely over, and stranded in the wake of this mass exodus are some once-thriving towns falling into ruin.

Bertha Ackerly (b. 1898)

BERTHA WORKING ON ONE OF HER "LOG CABIN" QUILTS IN 1985. PHOTOGRAPH COURTESY OF THE ERPF CATSKILL CULTURAL CENTER'S FOLKLIFE PROGRAM.

$\mathcal{O}$ne of the original six inductees in the Hall of Fame in 1982, Bertha Ackerly was the epitome of the old-time Catskill Mountains quiltmaker. Born on Thunder Hill in 1898, Bertha moved to Grahamsville in Sullivan County in 1923, where she and her husband started a dairy farm with "seven cows and a pair of horses." Eking out an existence from the hard life of a small farm, Bertha and her husband weathered the Great Depression and all of the many changes wrought on farm life by the twentieth century. And they prospered. As the farm grew to 150 cows, Bertha's family grew as well. First, three children, followed by eight grandchildren, and finally seventeen great-grandchildren—and each new arrival was greeted with a quilt, handmade by Bertha.

"When 'quilting day' arrives and Bertha isn't present I know she's either very (and I mean very) ill or away on a trip," wrote Kathleen Rolfs in 1982 when she sponsored Bertha Ackerly's nomination for the Hall of Fame. In the days when candidates themselves directly applied to the Hall of Fame, Bertha was the first to be elected without her knowledge. Perhaps a characteristic modesty is the reason Bertha did not come forward herself. She was to say a couple of years later, "I don't think there's much of an artist about me." Her peers disagreed. And so had the judges at the Grahamsville Fair, year after year. As Kathleen Rolfs wrote in 1982, "Whenever she shows them at the fair she receives first prize. Last year she received a special award on one and blue ribbons on the others."

Bertha Ackerley's quiltmaking nearly spanned the twentieth century. When she was only eleven or twelve years old she was taught to piece by an older sister. By the age of fourteen, she was quilting. She learned perfectionism from that first instruction: "I'll never forget it because I think I ripped it out as many times as I put it together. Every time I'd get a corner that didn't match, she'd make me take it out. If I had stitches that were too long, I had to take them out." The high standards instilled during that early training stayed with Bertha all of her life. She was to state in 1985, after nearly three quarters of a century making quilts: "Perfect quiltmanship. That, in my estimation, is what makes a good quilter ... If I can't do it right, I don't want to do it."

No one knows how many quilts were made by Bertha, although "everyone agrees it would have to be over one hundred" [Kathleen Rolfs, 1982]. For over thirty years, right up until the time of her death, she was a steadfast member of the Claryville Ladies Aid Society which meets once a week at the Reformed Church to tie or quilt tops. Bertha was an informal instructor within that group, never tiring of encouraging others and sharing her expertise. "She does not applique, although I've seen her show friends how to do it," wrote Kathleen Rolfs in 1982. "She prefers piecing and quilting." And the quality of that piecing? "Perfect," wrote Kathleen.

Diane Atkins (b. 1952)

THE 72" BY 72" BED QUILT, "IMMIGRANT'S DREAM," WAS MADE FOR THE 1986 CENTENNIAL OF THE STATUE OF LIBERTY. PIECED AND APPLIQUED, USING POLISHED COTTON, HAND-QUILTED AND FEATURING THE LYRICS TO "AMERICA THE BEAUTIFUL" EMBROIDERED IN CHAINSTITCH AROUND THE BORDER, IT WAS MADE BY DIANE "BEFORE I LEARNED HOW TO QUILT," SHE SAID. THE INNER BORDER OF "PINWHEEL" BLOCKS REPRESENT THE SIGNAL FLAGS OF SHIPS CARRYING IMMIGRANTS TO THE NEW WORLD. DIANE IS WEARING A QUILTED VEST SHE "FOOT-QUILTED" (DIANE'S PREFERRED TERM FOR MACHINE-QUILTING).

"*I*'m a rule-breaker," Diane stated at the very start of the interview at her home in Liberty, Sullivan County. "I'm not serious. I just have fun. It's an expression of my personality." And a unique personality it is, one that enters into every one of her quilts. Diane does not need to sign her work; the signature is already there. A playful spirit inhabits and informs her art, as evidenced in some of the titles themselves: "The Clintons Rock the White House," "Electromagnetic Fields," "Reagan's Star Wars." Asked to define her quiltmaking (is it fine art or folk art?), Diane responded, "It's just me. That's a piece of my personality out there. But it's one that everybody can reach out and shake hands with."

One of the new breed of quiltmakers who has come to the craft from a fine arts background, Diane quickly dispelled any notion that she is a stereotypical "artistic" quilter. She does not make her quilts with white glove treatment in mind. "My dogs stay on them," she said with a laugh. "I've got one on my couch. This weekend my nephew used one of my quilts for a saddle blanket and he won a blue ribbon at the horse show." And she is a staunch defender of quiltmaking as a folk art, "because it's an art form for everybody. Anybody who wants to be creative–you take up quilting, and you are. What's quilting if everybody can't do it?"

Diane was born in Suffern, NY, and moved to Liberty at the age of seven when her father was hired to run the greenhouse at Grossinger's resort. Her mother taught her (and her brother) to sew and embroider, but Diane's heart was not in it. "I hated Home Ec.," she laughed. Instead, Diane's passions became painting and drawing, particularly pen and ink sketches. But then in the mid-1980s Diane began to suffer from nervous problems: "The doctor said I was on the verge of a nervous breakdown. He suggested I take up needlework."

She followed the doctor's orders, beginning with counted cross-stitch, quickly moving on to quiltmaking. She made her first full-size quilt for the Statue of Liberty centennial in 1986. "I had no idea what I was doing," she said. Self-taught up to that point, Diane then met Beatrice Rexford, one of the area's most influential and respected quilting teachers: "She told me I was doing it all wrong. But I sent it to the State Fair anyway and won second prize. For my very first quilt."

Diane's friendship with Bea Rexford grew from that point on, and Diane became one of the charter members of the Calico Geese quilting guild which Ms. Rexford was in the process of starting up. Later she served as president of the guild. Quiltmaking became a way for Diane to incorporate her love of drawing with the relaxation of sewing. Her specialty is original quilting designs, which she draws on the top in washable ink. She also started a mail order business from her home selling original patterns for beginners—color-coded applique-by-number designs—and has received orders from as far away as Australia and Turkey.

For all of Diane's lack of pretense, her playful spirit and unorthodox approach to the art, make no mistake about the quality of her work. Diane taught herself to quilt in 1986. A mere six years later she was chosen by her peers for induction into the Hall of Fame. Art does not have to be ponderous to be brilliant. There is room for the whimsical, even the irreverent. In the summer of 1993 Diane was working on "The Ultimate Mermaid," a wholecloth quilt for her husband. The quilt was laid out on a large frame suspended from the living room ceiling by pulleys. It is lowered at night to a level just above the couch where Diane sits on her "couch quilt" and stitches along the lines of the patterns she drew of mermaids, whales and sea horses. It is a remarkable work in every way—in conception, design, execution, perseverance.

It is also a remarkable amount of work. But the rewards go beyond the finished product. "When you're quilting, everything disappears and you can be yourself. There's no pressure. It's the repetition. Your mind empties. It's a stress release. It's very soothing. And doctors recommend it." [Diane Atkins, 1993]

Martha Denman (b. 1903)

MARTHA WORKING ON A "MAPLE LEAF" QUILT IN 1985. PHOTOGRAPH COURTESY OF THE ERPF CATSKILL CULTURAL CENTER'S FOLKLIFE PROGRAM.

"*Quilting* is more or less an art anymore," says Martha Denman, who well remembers the days when quiltmaking was merely another chore in the daily rounds of a farmer's wife. Martha's mother, like most rural women at the turn of the century—and certainly almost all farm wives—fulfilled all of her family's clothing needs by the industry of her own hands. And any remnants left over were carefully saved to make quilts. "Of course," Martha adds, "she couldn't do the quilts to show or anything like that. She did it more for the need of them. She tied most of them." But sometimes they were quilted. Martha remembers that her mother did get pleasure from quiltmaking even though "at that time she had to sew. You didn't go out to the store and buy everything you needed like you would today."

Those quilts are gone now, as is the small farm in Neversink where Martha spent her early days. The fields where Martha played as a child are deep under the Rondout Reservoir, the entire valley drowned to help slake New York City's thirst. Soon after she married, Martha and her husband moved to South Kortright in Delaware County where they purchased a dairy farm with "about a hundred cows. It was rough, but we managed to get along," Martha recalls. Then World War II made it impossible to maintain a farm of that size in thinly-populated Delaware County: "You couldn't get any kind of help that you could depend on at all. So we finally got rid of it."

The Denmans moved back to Sullivan County and bought a smaller farm in Grahamsville, one that they could manage themselves without hired hands. But over the years the smaller farms became unviable as well. "Farming down here isn't anything," Martha said. "It got so milk was so cheap and there was restrictions on it. You had to do this, you had to do that. Why bother? If you didn't have anything left from your milk check after paying your feed bill, what're you working for?" Martha still lives on that farm, which her son continues to operate on a limited basis.

It was on that first large farm in South Kortright that Martha began to quilt. She had learned sewing and embroidery from her mother, but it wasn't until she was carrying her first daughter that she turned her skills to quiltmaking. With no instruction ("I just figured it out"), Martha pieced a top in nine-inch blocks and embroidered it with nursery rhyme scenes for her unborn daughter. Two more daughters were born in the ensuing years, but for each child—and their mother—that first quilt always remained the favorite.

Many more quilts were to follow. As for favorite patterns, Martha once said, "There are hundreds of them that I like the best," although in later years Martha developed a particular fondness for "Cathedral Windows." Martha liked to piece, applique or quilt at home in the quiet of the evening. For companionship she joined the venerable Claryville Ladies Aid Society. She worked with them for many years quilting tops to benefit the Reformed Church, as the Society has done continuously for literally longer than anyone can remember.

Now at the age of ninety, Martha Denman looks out on the world with eyes that have witnessed almost a century of the slow and inexorable decline in the fortunes of agriculture in the Catskills. Those eyes have become weary with time and, sadly, too weakened by the 1990s to continue her quilted art. "It got so it bothered my eyes too much to quilt," Martha explained. "When the light is bright, then I can sew what I need to, but I don't do quilting anymore." She still visits with her friends in Claryville; "I enjoy quilts and seeing the work they do," but "all I'm getting out of it is the pleasure of it, so why strain my eyes?" [Martha Denman, 1993]

Beatrice Rexford (b. 1930)

THE LARGE BED QUILT (MIDWAY BETWEEN A DOUBLE AND A QUEEN) WAS
HAND-PIECED AND HAND-QUILTED BY BEA AND HER STUDENTS AS A TEACH-
ING TOOL. IT WAS BEGUN IN THE EARLY 1980S AND FINALLY COMPLETED IN
1995. TITLED "BEA'S PERENNIAL QUILT," IT WAS CONSTRUCTED FROM SCRAPS
SAVED BY BEA AND HER STUDENTS. EACH "CHIMNEY" IN THE CENTER OF
EACH BLOCK OF THIS "BARN RAISING" PATTERN IS DIFFERENT, PROVIDED BY
A DIFFERENT STUDENT DURING THE LONG ONGOING CONSTRUCTION OF THE
QUILT.

"There are very few native Sullivan County people," Beatrice Rexford explained. "People have moved on. People have moved in." But Bea Rexford's ancestors came to stay. One side of Bea's family traces its lineage all the way back to the original Hardenberghs who laid claim to an estimated two million acres of Catskill Mountain land through the Great Patent of 1708. "But I don't have anything to show for it," Bea said with a laugh. As her other great-grandfather was part Native American, Bea Rexford may very well descend from both sides of that famous (or infamous) 300-year-old real estate transaction.

Bea Rexford was born in 1930 on a dairy farm in Hasbrouck, a tiny hamlet in Sullivan County near the Ulster County border. It was a time when diversity of employment and extended families were a way of life in the Catskills. Her grandparents lived in one wing of the rambling farmhouse, and part of the downstairs doubled as a general store and post office. Bea fondly remembers growing up with her grandparents always near at hand, and her love for quilts stems from those memories. "Grandma always had quilts," Bea recalls, "and I knew if I were sick or whatever, if I got to Grandma's ... and I could get in that bed with that old 'Log Cabin' quilt on the top, that I would be perfectly, perfectly safe. And I still feel about quilts that way."

Quilts were a part of everyday life in Sullivan County in the 1930s. "We always had them," Bea said. "Back in my grandmother's generation everybody had quilts." Bea remembers how the Ladies Aid Society of the Reformed Church in nearby Claryville would make a quilt as a going-away present for "the circuit riders and the old ministers" when they moved on to another parish.

Bea started to make her own quilts—miniatures for her dolls—when she was very young, without having received any real instruction. Neither grandmother (both of whom were quiltmakers), nor her mother, actually taught her how to piece and quilt; she learned by watching. But the basics of sewing were a standard item in a girl's education in the 1930s, and Bea further benefited from the expertise within her own family. In addition to the talents of the two grandmothers, Bea's mother "was a fantastic crocheter," Bea said, and Sunday afternoons were given to home lessons in dressmaking, knitting and embroidery.

Bea continued to use those sewing skills through her teens and, indeed, through all of her adult life, but she would not return to quiltmaking until the early 1970s. Her life was just too busy until then. Bea had married and moved to Hurleyville, where she raised six children while working full-time as a registered nurse. But she never stopped saving scraps of fabric, and when her children were in their teens, the opportunity arose to begin to use those remnants. Looking back to the early 1970s, Bea recalls her tentative—and thrifty—return to the art: "Before there were any books or anything out, I would sit in my nursery where I was working, and I would take graph paper and I would sketch out something in six-inch blocks, and I would make it. And if I liked it, I knew I could make it in a twelve-inch block. And if I didn't like it especially, I knew it was the right size for a potholder and wouldn't be wasted."

While in the course of filling her kitchen with a lifetime's supply of potholders, Bea completed her first bed quilt, a full-size "Log Cabin"—an obvious tribute to the warm memories Bea retained from her childhood. And that quilt was to accrue another layer of family memories because of the materials that went into it. Constructed like an antique quilt from scraps of clothing fabric collected over the years, it is a family history told in cloth. "It had in it all of my maternity clothes' fabric, the girls' square dance fabrics, all of their 4-H projects, all that sort of thing," Bea explained. "Every time the kids come home, they all say [looking at that quilt] 'Remember when you wore that. Remember when we had that.' That's my memory quilt."

More quilts (and potholders) were to follow as Bea Rexford continued to work on her own. Then the mid-1970s brought a sudden burgeoning interest in quiltmaking, and Bea found herself at the center of the quiltmaking revival in the lower Catskills. Through the late 1970s and early 1980s, Bea shared her self-taught skills by teaching quiltmaking at the Cornell Cooperative Extension in Liberty. Out of those classes grew the Calico Geese Quilters of Sullivan County, a quilting guild founded by Bea Rexford in 1986. With eighty members, the Calico Geese is the second largest guild in the Catskills. Bea also joined the Ulster County guild, Wiltwyck, and the two large guilds entered into an era of mutual cooperation, with some members active in both guilds and each guild drawing other members from as far away as Greene and Delaware counties. Quiltmaking in the Catskills became a regional activity with a growing sense of cohesion among its proponents.

And Bea Rexford was becoming recognized as one of the leaders within that community. Her work with the Cooperative Extension and the Calico Geese had helped galvanize quiltmaking activity throughout Sullivan County, and her influence spread even further through her participation in Wiltwyck and the Catskill Mountain Quilters Hall of Fame.

Growing up during the Depression left an indelible mark on Bea's later life. She still prefers using fabric remnants for her quilt tops, a carryover from her childhood when "we always had to make do with everything." The 1990s are much more affluent times but, for Bea, the process is the same. "Everybody gives me their scraps," she says. "After every class, when every little tidbit is left over, I always take those tidbits and make something out of them." In Bea Rexford's opinion nothing has really changed. Quilts, she says, are "made exactly the way today that they were back then. They still have to put them together piece by piece."

Bea Rexford is a traditionalist in every sense. She believes quilts are meant to be used. She doesn't make quilted wall-hangings because "a wall doesn't need to be warm. So I don't see the point." And it is not as though Bea Rexford does not know the value quilts can acquire. She helped document and catalog the antique quilt collection of the Sullivan County Historical Society for the Museum of American Folk Art in 1989. But for Bea Rexford, the real value of quilts has nothing to do with museum collections, blue ribbons or high price tags. "I give them to people," she says. "I never will sell any of them. I give them to you if I love you, but I won't sell them because there's too much of me in them. I love to see the grandchildren drag them. I don't care if they're loved to tatters; that's exactly what they're for." [Bea Rexford, 1993]

Kathleen Rolfs (b. 1913)

THE DOUBLE-SIZED BED QUILT WAS MADE FOR KATHLEEN BY HER DAUGHTER-IN-LAW FROM PICTURES DRAWN BY KATHLEEN'S GRANDCHILDREN. IT WAS HAND-APPLIQUED AND HAND-QUILTED, AND COMPLETED IN 1975.

*W*hen Kathleen Rolfs first joined the Claryville Reformed Church, the congregation in the winter months could dwindle to only six people. In the summers the church would fill with vacationers from resorts and seasonal homes. The steady faithful six would then be scattered in a crowd of comparatively affluent New Yorkers. One year, a summer visitor asked Kathleen why the church didn't have a choir. Kathleen replied, "Well, when I came here we had to decide whether we wanted a congregation or a choir. The congregation won out. We had to have somebody sitting in the front there." By the 1990s, the winter congregation had burgeoned to twenty.

Claryville is a magical place, easier to spot on the map than from your car. One can drive past it several times—no great feat—before realizing it was there. Claryville is nestled in a narrow stream-fed valley in northern Sullivan County. The surrounding hills rise precipitously on either side of the proud little church and its well-tended graveyard. Across the road is the church hall where every Thursday members of the Ladies Aid gather to quilt tops to benefit the church, an activity of the Society which has been going on for longer than anyone knows. "I don't know exactly when they started," Kathleen said. "I tried to find out, but I couldn't." Claryville is almost too good to be true—and the residents know it. "I can't picture myself living anywhere else," Kathleen remarked.

Kathleen was born in 1913 on her grandfather's hilltop farm near Grahamsville, a small village only a few miles from Claryville. Her mother was an immigrant from Ireland who had settled in Manhattan. She loved the city and hated the country, while Kathleen's father was "a country boy," Kathleen said, who "couldn't stand" New York City. The "compromise" they worked out was to live in Manhattan, and Kathleen spent the first thirteen years of her life there. Her mother's death, when Kathleen was only eight years old, was to cause a succession of moves which would eventually lead Kathleen Rolfs, at age sixteen, back to Grahamsville.

The Grahamsville area in the late 1920s had a strong and active quiltmaking tradition. "Everybody up here made quilts at that time," Kathleen remarked. "It was a necessity." Her father had re-married by then, and it was Kathleen's stepmother who would introduce her to quiltmaking. "What we made was just quilts for the beds," Kathleen said. "We didn't put them in picture frames." All the quilts were made to be used, but there were two distinct categories of quilts: "utility" quilts and "best" quilts. The utility quilts were "ugly quilts," Kathleen said, "made out of old coats and things like that ... anything we had to keep warm. We made a lot of those. All tied. You couldn't possibly quilt anything with materials as heavy as that." Making those utility quilts was a chore. They were slapped together quickly from materials at hand, without art or embellishment. "We were mountain people and we were very poor, and also the Depression came along eventually," Kathleen explained, but "of course, we didn't know the difference. We'd always been poor."

Kathleen and her stepmother would look forward to the time when they had saved enough money to buy new fabric from itinerant peddlers. They could then start on a "nice quilt" which would be pieced into a pattern and quilted. Working on the "nice quilts" was "a big thrill," Kathleen said, but that pleasure was earned at the expense of doing without in some other area. As Kathleen continued, "I think for the young people who have so much it's very hard to understand, but when we bought nice material to make nice quilts that you quilted on, you sacrificed something else." Quilting a top pieced from fresh new material was a special treat, and Kathleen and her stepmother would carefully sort through the peddler's wares, picking out "nice patterns to make a nice quilt." Those few hard-earned, hard-saved dollars bought many hours of pleasure: "We used to have wonderful times quilting together," Kathleen said.

Kathleen thus occupied the spare hours of the remainder of her teen years quilting with her stepmother. But at age twenty life changed again. Kathleen married, became a mother and "didn't make any quilts for years," she said. After sixteen years of marriage Kathleen's husband died, leaving Kathleen to support and finish raising her two children on her own. Those were difficult years but, proud and resilient, Kathleen survived, taking whatever employment was available to keep food on the table. Eventually she secured the position of postmaster for Claryville, which gave her "a lot of free time." She began to bring to work bags of fabric scraps she had saved for the past twenty years from the remnants left over from making clothes and curtains. When there were no customers, Kathleen would sit in the back of the post office piecing those scraps together into a quilt top.

Kathleen continued making quilts on her own for the next twenty years. The children left home to start families and careers, and Kathleen began her own life anew, re-marrying and retiring, determined "not to do a thing," as she said. But Kathleen claims to have a large "V" (for "volunteer") emblazoned on her forehead. She began to become active in civics groups, and her husband suggested she join the Ladies Aid of the Claryville Reformed Church. Kathleen responded, "You think I'm going to go down there and sit with those old ladies? Not on your life!"

But she finally did join, in 1970, "kicking and screaming" as she would later recall. "I was the baby then [at age fifty-seven]," Kathleen said. Although Kathleen had been making quilts for over forty years, "It was made very plain to me ... that I didn't know an awful lot about quilting, and I didn't have too much clout there." The Claryville Ladies Aid was, indeed, venerable and accomplished. They had been quilting tops to benefit their small church for generations. And they *were* old. A couple of years after Kathleen joined, the Society ceased operating for a short while because too many members had died, lost their sight or become too enfeebled by age. The "baby" of the group, with the "V" on her forehead, stepped in. Kathleen agreed to accept the presidency of the Ladies Aid, providing, she said, "they throw the rule book out the window."

They agreed, and throw it she did. She opened up membership in the Society to anyone who wanted to join, regardless of religious affiliation, ability—or even whether that person was interested in quilt-making at all. Some members attend each week just to watch, join in the conversation and laughter, or help with lunch. Kathleen Rolfs is justly proud of what she calls her "United Nations Ladies." "We are Catholic, Jewish, Protestant—even Japanese," she says. Attendance varies seasonally, as it does in the church across the street. An average Thursday finds ten to fifteen women present. They finish an average of ten quilts a year, with all the proceeds going to the church. For the past nineteen years Kathleen Rolfs has presided each Thursday as "the only officer," she says. "My title is 'leader.'"

The Claryville Ladies Aid charges $200 to quilt a top. Even at ten quilts a year, the proceeds from their quilting cannot entirely support the church. But like a storybook ending, two substantial bequests have recently been left to support the little church and its steady congregation of twenty souls. Those bequests were given directly to the Ladies Aid for administration in recognition of their more than eighty years of service to the church, their steadfastness, their diligence and their fiscal responsibility.

Kathleen Rolfs does not like rules, but she certainly has standards that she will not deviate from. If you want a top quilted to give as a gift to friend or family, then contact the Claryville Ladies Aid. But, for Kathleen, quilts are not made for profit: "I absolutely refuse to do quilts for anybody that's going to sell them," she states.

And Kathleen, though tolerant of how others make quilts ("Machine-quilting is coming in very strong right now, and it's fine," she says), has very definite ideas of what a quilt should be. "The sewing machine is just a 'white elephant' in my house," she says. "To me it's an art, and you do it by hand." Unlike most traditional quilters, Kathleen does not even use the sewing machine to join blocks together or to apply the binding. All of her quilt tops are pieced; she does not like to applique, perhaps as a holdover from her teen years when she pieced and quilted with her step-mother who "wouldn't have the faintest idea how to applique."

Next to the church hall where the Claryville Ladies Aid meets is a restored one-room schoolhouse. Kathleen Rolfs helps administer the schoolhouse, and she conducts tours when groups visit. The entire complex of church, church hall, cemetery and schoolhouse sits alone on one bend of a county road, enclosed by towering hills. The road that passes follows a streambed through a clove in the foothills and leads directly to the heart of the Catskill Mountains. Entering Claryville, on that bend in the road, you briefly return to a past world, a better world, something that feels almost like home. Kathleen Rolfs and Claryville are so attuned to each other that it is hard to imagine one without the other. But her second husband's death brought a new intimation of mortality to Kathleen. Faced with moving to a smaller home in 1993, Kathleen stated, "I have boxes and boxes of [fabric] material. I thought I was going to live forever." So she has been bringing those boxes of material to share with her "United Nations Ladies" on Thursdays. But some of the constants in her life remain unchanged. As Kathleen said in closing, "The church and the Ladies Aid and the schoolhouse is all a part of me. It's strange to think that some day I'm going to leave it." [Kathleen Rolfs, 1993]

Connie Stangel (b. 1924)

THE 82" BY 94" BED QUILT WAS MACHINE-PIECED AND HAND-QUILTED BY CONNIE, COMPLETED IN 1995. FROM A MAGAZINE PATTERN, "RAVEN DANCE," INSPIRED BY THE NATIVE NORTH AMERICANS OF QUEEN CHARLOTTE ISLAND, CANADA, IT IS A VARIATION OF THE "PINWHEEL" PATTERN.

$\mathscr{C}$onnie Stangel did not begin to make quilts until 1969-1970, but her childhood in the 1920s and 1930s instilled in her the quiltmaker's traits of thrift and resourcefulness. She has always lived in the Catskills, but she spent each of her early summers at her maternal grandparents' farm in Pennsylvania. It was on that farm that we may see Connie Stangel's character and talents begin to emerge, as she later remembered:

> ... because being out at the farm in the summertime, from 15 to 20 miles [from the nearest village], and you only had a horse and wagon to get you someplace way back then, because my grandfather was—well, finally he learned to drive, but he was the worst driver in the world. And we used to go to the creamery with him on the horse and wagon every month. But you learned to be very frugal and very resourceful, and you could just about take anything and learn how to make it into whatever you wanted to make it into. That's the way I grew up.

Consequently, Connie says, "I'm a doer. I can't just sit and do nothing."

Her father's family was from Brown's Station in Ulster County, one of many Catskill Mountains villages to eventually disappear under the waters of New York City's reservoir system. Ironically, Connie's father worked for the Board of Water Supply, which kept him employed throughout the Depression years and thus kept his family from feeling the full effects of the economic calamity surrounding them. His job kept them on the move, giving Connie an early taste of the variety of the Catskills as they relocated from Gilboa to Grand Gorge, Tannersville, Kingston, Ellenville, finally settling for good in Sullivan County.

Both of Connie's grandmothers were quiltmakers, but both died when Connie was very young, so she never had the opportunity to watch them work. But the childhood memories of sleeping under their quilts never left her. In the early 1970s, Connie was touring Europe when she looked down at an old tiled floor and said, "That's Grandma's quilt!" When she returned to her home in Neversink, Sullivan County, she carefully replicated the quilt she remembered. "It's similar to the 'Snowball' [pattern]," Connie says, "but I just call it 'Mosaic,' 'cause there's sixty zillion of those [pieces in the quilt]."

That tribute to her grandmother (and to an anonymous tiler) was only Connie's second quilt. Her first quilt, made a couple of years previously, was a "Rail Fence" she copied from a magazine. "I just decided I wanted to make a quilt," she says, matter-of-factly, "so I made it." When she finished the top she tied it, because at that time, she says, "I was never gonna quilt a whole quilt." Connie doesn't recall any great difficulty in making those first two quilts entirely on her own, without lessons or instructions. But they were constructed after nearly forty years of "doing," of not sitting idly. She had learned sewing from her mother and, as a young mother herself, she sewed most of her daughters' dresses and most of her own clothes–not because she had to, but because it gave her pleasure. She could crochet and embroider, cane chairs, re-upholster and refinish furniture. She is also an accomplished amateur painter.

In fact, Connie incorporated painting in her quiltmaking long before it became fashionable. In the early 1970s, she painted a wild turkey on a plain white sheet and quilted it for one of her sons. For one of her daughters she used the same process, but with painted wildflowers. She made another quilt using her kindergarten students' crayon drawings, and recently made one for her granddaughter whose "pictures were all in magic markers," Connie explains, "so I had to put them on the window and trace around them and re-paint them."

Not all of Connie's earlier quilts were experimental, but since she was self-taught, each new quilt was still a voyage into uncharted depths because she did not want to repeat herself. She started to watch for designs in magazines and made quilts with classic patterns, such as "Nine-Block," "Around the World," "Log Cabin," "Fan Quilt," and "Winner's Circle."

Finally, around 1984-85, Connie took a course in quiltmaking from Bea Rexford at the Cooperative Extension in Liberty. ("After I made 25 or more quilts, I decided I better take a course," she says.) Aside from learning new techniques, the course benefited Connie by introducing her to the growing community of quiltmakers. She became one of the charter members of the Calico Geese and went on to become an instructor herself, teaching workshops within the guild and a series of courses at the Tri-Valley Adult Education Center.

Perhaps because she is still basically self-taught, Connie's quilting method is unorthodox. "I can't use a frame," she says. "It kills my back." Instead, Connie spreads the quilt on her floor, stretches one area at a time with her hoop frame and pins it closely. She removes the hoop and quilts that one small pinned area, and then repeats the whole process over and over until the entire quilt is quilted. "I suppose mine get a little more puffy than these people that put them on a quilt frame," Connie admits, adding, "but I happen to like them that way."

"I do it [quiltmaking] because I like it, and I do just as I please," Connie says. She has won ribbons at shows, but she does not make quilts to win ribbons. She sold one quilt, but she never makes a quilt with a buyer in mind. She makes whichever quilt is in her heart to make at any given time. The majority of her quilted works—full-size, crib quilts, wall-hangings and miniatures—are given to family and friends. Two memorable quilts were made for two members of her church who were struggling with AIDS and alcoholism, respectively. She is proud of the work her guild does for needful local families. For Connie Stangel, "doing" and "giving" are closely aligned.

She still returns to the farm in Pennsylvania, although not for the whole summer. Like many of the farms in her native Catskills, Connie's ancestral farm is dormant. The barns became dilapidated and were taken down a few years ago. Keeping up with the grounds and maintenance has become a constant burden. But it remains in the family, and it helps keep the memories alive.

Recently, Connie repaired an antique quilt—a "Bear Claw" pattern in white and "turkey red" which her grandmother had pieced and her great-aunt had quilted in 1910. Saving that quilt was another way to keep the memories alive. Like most other Catskill Mountains quilt-makers, Connie wants the majority of her work to stay in the family, heirlooms to preserve the present into the future. It is a legacy of frugality and resourcefulness, of using instead of wasting, of doing and making-do, because "that's the way I grew up," she says.

"Alphabet Quilt" by Theresa Scheetz. The 36" by 50" crib quilt was hand-appliqued, machine-pieced and hand-quilted by Theresa in 1985/1986 as a gift for her newborn niece. The pattern was modified from a pieced antique quilt Theresa had seen in a book.

CHAPTER 6

Greene County

*H*alf valley, half mountaintop, Greene County is neatly bisected by the northeastern escarpment of the Catskills. From the valley below, the mountains appear to rise abruptly, majestically, belying their relatively modest stature.

The sheer cliffs level off at one spot near the top to form a small tableland, a little meadow actually, which became known as the Pine Orchard. It was there the Catskill Mountain House stood for a century and a half, joined for a time by the Hotel Kaaterskill (a little higher up, a little grander). In the 1800s, steamship passengers on the Hudson River could look up to see lights from the hotels' candelabrum shining high up among the clouds. Later stargazers could see, reportedly from as far away as Massachusetts, the flames that engulfed the two landmarks.

Geographically and culturally diverse, Greene boasts mountain hamlets with English names and old river towns with Dutch names, testifying to the later settlement of the higher elevations.

Greene's glory days, in retrospect, were in the mid-nineteenth century, when Thomas Cole lived in Catskill and painted the environs, collecting about him disciples who later congregated in Palenville for

119

easier access to the mountain wilds, giving that hamlet a brief reign as an artists colony. His most successful follower, Frederic Church, built his home directly across the Hudson River, in Columbia County, because the view was better from there.

The village of Catskill had a brief resurgence in favorite son civic pride in the 1980s when Cus D'Amato's gym above the police station began to churn out world-class boxers, most notably Mike Tyson. But that recognition and hometown boosterism has faded away like the billboards at the entrances to the village that once proudly proclaimed "The Home of Mike Tyson."

An unintentional sort of tug-of-war for tourist dollars has existed for over a century between mountaintop and valley. As the grand hotel era faded on the mountaintop, family farms in the valley converted to family summer resorts and thrived during the middle years of this century. As they, in turn, waned in popularity (many of them neglected and targets for arson, or converted into tax-exempt camps), the ski areas in the mountains began to grow and prosper.

Albany County lies to the north, Ulster County to the south, and those residents with both marketable skills and a reliable car commute to Albany or Kingston for employment. Those with one or the other, but not both, may still find employment, at least seasonally, in the so-called "hospitality" industry catering to the needs of travelers and vacationers—Greene's role from as early as the turnpike days.

Pauline Lawrence (b. 1921)

PAULINE LAWRENCE WITH HER GRANDDAUGHTER. PHOTOGRAPH BY JOSEPH
LEVY, 1991. COLLECTION OF BLACK DOME PRESS.

*H*ad Pauline Lawrence never touched a needle and thread, she would still be one of the most remarkable people in the Catskill Mountains. Quiltmaking is only one of her many skills. She believes in self-sufficiency, in knowing how to do things for herself. Were there to be another Great Depression, Pauline Lawrence would be almost unaffected. "The young people today, I feel sorry for them in a way," Pauline says, "because there's so many things they don't know. They don't know how to survive."

Pauline's ancestors were among the first settlers to come to the mountaintop wilderness of what is now the Windham/Ashland area in Greene County, arriving from Connecticut in the mid-1700s. They found a rugged frontier encircled by the high peaks of the Catskills, shunned even by the Indians as being too inhospitable for permanent settlement. But Pauline's ancestors came with the skills to survive in that climate and terrain. They carved farms out of the forest and lived off the land. If they needed anything, they made it themselves. Nine generations later, Pauline's family retains many of those skills.

Pauline still lives in the farmhouse in Ashland in which she was born in 1921. By then, the mountaintop was already changing from an agrarian economy, with some light manufacturing, to a resort economy, but Pauline's family continued to work the land as their ancestors had done. Having retained the land and the skills to work it, Pauline's family lived through the Depression as though it never occurred. "We always canned and froze everything that we had to eat," she says. "We never bought much of anything. You bought flour by the barrel. Sugar by fifty pounds. And that was stored and you made your own bread. You lived off the land."

The family worked together to survive. On a small farm in the Catskills in the 1930s there was less differentiation between chores done by women and those done by men than many people today would presume. Pauline's father (and his father before him) drove the stagecoach between Hunter and Ashland in the winters. "Then in the summertime my mother drove," Pauline explained. And children, regardless of gender, were expected to do their part. "I used to get up four o'clock in the morning and milk cows," Pauline said. "And we used to have a tractor, and in the spring I had to get up at least five o'clock and go over and harrow the fields until school bus time."

Part of surviving independently meant the family had to hand-make their own bedcoverings. Pauline was only four years old when her grandmother taught her to cut out one-inch-square pieces from fabric remnants and sew the pieces together into quilt tops. She was then taught to put a sheet between the finished top and the backing and to quilt it together into a doll or crib quilt. It would have been unthought-of to use new materials for a quilt, so "you worked with what you had," Pauline explained. They saved every flour, sugar and feed bag, which usually became the backing for a quilt. "The economy was the basic thing," Pauline added. Material included recycled fabrics from dresses and aprons, "anything that was not completely worn out." And Pauline remembers that "way, way back they used to put newspapers in between" for the batting, though that practice had died out by the time Pauline was a child.

The continuous labor and hard work necessary to maintain a self-supporting mountain farm in the 1930s did not prevent Pauline's family from contributing to their community. Her grandmother was president of the Ladies Auxiliary for the Ashland Presbyterian Church, and Pauline remembers attending their quilting bees when she was a child. Pauline's mother used to tie small wool and corduroy "crazy quilts" to donate to wheelchair patients for use as lap blankets. No matter how busy they were, Pauline's industrious family always found time to help others through the difficult years.

Pauline continued the family tradition of reaching out to the community when she began to teach for the Cornell Cooperative Extension in 1953. After taking a series of courses at Cornell in a variety of home arts, including upholstering, refinishing furniture, making draperies, braiding rugs, caning chairs, rushing seats, etc., Pauline spent the next twenty years traveling throughout Greene and Columbia counties teaching those skills in workshops which were "held in firehouses, in church halls. You used to lug all your equipment around," she recalls.

All of that activity, and the mastering of one craft after another, prevented Pauline until the 1970s from returning to the quiltmaking arts she had learned as a child, but her interest in quiltmaking never waned. "I always admired everybody else's work," she says. "I used to go to quilt shows. But I felt that I just didn't have the time, and until I did I didn't want to get into it." Pauline was too much of a perfectionist to begin any project unless she could devote the amount of time needed to do it right. After retiring from the Extension program in the early 1970s, Pauline finally had the time to return to quiltmaking and she has averaged at least one quilt per year ever since. She never sells her quilts. They are all given away to family or donated to charities. "I try to give each one of the churches in the area something that I have made that they can use, raffle off or sell in their sales, or whatever they do," she states.

Pauline's quiltmaking is very traditional, as one might expect. Although her mother "wore out two sewing machines in her lifetime," Pauline prefers to piece and quilt by hand, using a sewing machine only for joining blocks together or adding the binding. She owns a small portable plastic frame, but she prefers to use her grandmother's large frame, wooden pegs and all, because "I like the whole thing laid out," she says. But one suspects the preference is partly sentimental, for Pauline remembers that frame from her childhood as being "always on the backs of the dining room chairs." She still makes most of her own clothes and saves the leftover fabric for her quilts. She has taught her granddaughter how to make quilts, just as her grandmother had taught her. The only real difference between Pauline's quiltmaking today and the quilts she made as a child is that today she prefers applique over piecing. In the 1920s and 1930s, as Pauline remembers, all of the tops were pieced.

Pauline is still willing to share the skills she has acquired with "anyone who wants to learn." Occasionally she gives demonstrations at Ski Windham or in public schools. She sometimes discovers an appalling ignorance about not only the arts she instructs but the very environment itself. "I used to go in and teach little things like making, say, pine cone wreaths with fourth graders," Pauline recalls. "And I felt so sorry for those children because some of them didn't even know what a pine cone is. And they live in the country!" Her only regularly-scheduled instruction is with The Golden Agers, a small group of retired women who meet once a week in Hensonville to learn quiltmaking.

Pauline's quilts are beautiful works of art, and through her instruction and sharing her skills she has enriched the art of quiltmaking in the Catskills. But Pauline's finest achievement, indeed the full flowering of a lifetime wisely spent mastering hand skills, is not to be found in her quilts. Behind the Lawrence farmhouse on Route 23 between Windham and Ashland is a large two-story barn filled with over fifty authentic antique carriages, each one perfectly restored ("and roadworthy," Pauline adds) from rusting and rotting wrecks discovered in barns and fields throughout the Catskills. When Pauline's husband could no longer work as an excavator, "he needed a hobby," Pauline stated, with characteristic understatement, "and that's how we got in the carriage business." To restore just one of those carriages would be a noteworthy achievement, requiring upholstery and leather-working talents, wood-refinishing and metal-working skills—and hundreds of hours of labor. For two retired people to restore fifty of them is no less than astounding. And each one looks like it just rolled out of a factory for the first time.

Pauline Lawrence's entire life has been lived undaunted by hard times or hard work. "When my husband got sick with cancer," she says, "we thought that many cancers, the different kinds, come from chemicals in food. So we raised our own food. We used to put up five hundred jars of all sorts of vegetables. I raised my own fish—rainbow trout. There's a little pond out in the back. It's fun." Now in her early seventies, Pauline Lawrence gives the impression that she would survive through virtually any adversity that could befall her. Were the world to run out of gasoline for its cars, or electricity for its lights and heat, or any of the other luxuries of the twentieth century, Pauline would survive, thrive and be quite content. "I still wish I lived in the horse and buggy days," she smiles.

Agnes Proper (b. 1900)

PHOTOGRAPH COURTESY OF THE ERPF CATSKILL CULTURAL CENTER'S
FOLKLIFE PROGRAM.

*W*hile he was curator of the Zadock Pratt Museum in 1984, Charles Proper made the comment about his mother Agnes that "she's made everything but shoes." But as it turns out, Agnes Proper *did* make a pair of shoes once. During a long and resourceful life, Agnes Proper tested her abilities in virtually every line of what she referred to as "handwork." "I just love to do it," she said in 1986, while she was a resident at the Cottone Home, a small adult care facility in Prattsville, Greene County. "I'd be right at it—quilts or whatever—now, if I could. I'd be happy as a lark."

Agnes Proper resided in the Catskill Mountains for all of her ninety-two years. She was born in 1900 on a farm in Breakabeen, near Blenheim in Schoharie County, and she was raised in the turn-of-the-century mountaintop tradition of hard work and self-sufficiency. But to that discipline was added a dash of art which raised the family's homemade products above the level of the merely functional. In an interview in 1986 Agnes remembered her mother's influence around the farmhouse, discovering grace and beauty in the most mundane objects: "My mother could take an old sugar bowl that was cracked. She'd put a ribbon on it, hang it up, and it was a pretty thing. I think people have an eye for something like that ... She could see the whole thing done once she started it."

Agnes's mother was not a quiltmaker however, and Agnes herself did not begin to make quilts until much later in her life, but she fondly recalled one of her aunts, Agnes Hager, who "always quilted." She remembered her Aunt Agnes entering the landmark Sears, Roebuck and Co. quilt contest at the 1933 World's Fair in Chicago, where she received an "honorable mention" among the field of 25,000 entrants. By that time, Agnes had married and moved to Downsville, near the Pepacton Reservoir in Delaware County, but the influence of her aunt stayed with her all of her life. From watching her aunt make quilts many years before, Agnes claimed she "knew how to do it" before she even started her own first quilt, a "Dresden Plate," in 1960.

Agnes was prompted to take up quiltmaking that year through the influence of friends she had made during the evening classes she taught in knitting and crocheting—arts she had practiced all her life. She began to attend "different quiltings around town" in the early 1960s, she said, and quiltmaking quickly became part of Agnes's daily routine. She would rise each morning and work on her quilts while the light was strong, putting up with the good-natured heckling of her husband who "couldn't understand anybody cutting up little pieces of good material and then putting it back together again."

A traditionalist at heart and a pragmatist, Agnes never forgot the lessons in frugality learned during her early years on that farm in Breakabeen. She preferred piecing with scrap material because the finished quilt would then "go with anything," she said. The multi-colored and variegated "Cathedral Windows" coverlet became her favorite style in later years. And she followed her mother's example by finding aesthetic use for everyday objects, even discovering, as she told Janis Benincasa in 1986, that men's white woolen underwear made a perfect background for hooked rugs.

Agnes Proper made only about a dozen quilts—but it is quality of workmanship, not number of works, that determines selection for the Hall of Fame. Agnes was an easy selection for induction in 1984. She had that quiltmaker's Midas's touch, turning scraps of fabric into intricate and harmonious objects of beauty.

Virginia Roberts (b. 1906)

PHOTOGRAPH 1985. COURTESY OF THE ERPF CATSKILL CULTURAL CENTER'S FOLKLIFE PROGRAM.

*I*n 1941, shortly before America's entry into World War II changed the course of history, Virginia Roberts entered some of her quilts for competition in the Mineola Fair on Long Island and won two blue ribbons. More than half a century later, in 1993, as America was closing military bases all over the world following the disintegration of the Soviet Union, Virginia submitted her latest quilt and won "Viewer's Choice" (an honor she had been awarded for the third year running) at the annual quilt and craft show of the Patchworkers guild in East Jewett. Some things don't change.

"My quilting days aren't very exciting," Virginia announced. "What I've done I've been pleased to do and I've enjoyed it, so I wouldn't change it ... [but] I don't make much anymore," she continued. "There isn't anything special to make it for, so I just don't bother." Having made over forty full-size quilts, as well as twenty crib quilts, Virginia's semi-retirement from quiltmaking is certainly understandable, especially considering that every one of those quilts was hand-pieced or hand-appliqued, and they were all hand-quilted. Her friendship with her fellow Patchworkers is now the motivating factor in her continuing involvement in quiltmaking. "It brings you closer to people who have the same interests and like to do what you like to do," Virginia explains. "You can share your ideas and thoughts with them."

Virginia Roberts was born in St. Louis in 1906. Her family relocated to the suburbs of New York City when Virginia was three, and she would spend the next sixty years there. While growing up on Long Island, Virginia learned the basics of dressmaking, embroidery, needlepoint and quiltmaking from her mother and grandmother—skills that she would employ during her leisure hours for the next eighty years.

Although she had learned quiltmaking at a much earlier age, Virginia didn't actually begin her first quilt until 1936 when she was in her late twenties and well-established in her dual careers of health teacher and registered nurse. The tranquility of quiltmaking appealed to Virginia after a tense shift in the operating room. She would look forward to her "handicraft work," as she termed it, as "things that relax you and take you away from things."

In later years Virginia would prefer applique patterns like "Ohio Rose," but in the 1930s and 1940s all of her quilt tops were pieced.

"Boston Commons" and "Ohio Star" were two of her favorites at that time; "I made two or three of each one of those," she states. To Virginia they were useful items made for a purpose, not delicate art objects to store away or hang on a wall. As she explained, "... a couple my husband used, he finally threw over his motorcycle to cover it. They got older, you know? But we used them, really used them in those days."

In 1972 Virginia and her husband, an ardent hunter and fisherman, retired and moved to the Catskill Mountains, settling in the community of East Jewett in Greene County. Virginia noticed right away that people on the mountaintop "seemed more interested in quilting." After forty years of making quilts on her own, Virginia joined the Patchworkers guild in 1976 and helped them construct their bicentennial quilt. "I've worked on a quilt with them every year since then," Virginia said in 1993. She also joined the Wiltwyck guild in Kingston, and her talents and many years of devotion to quilting were immediately recognized. Virginia Roberts was inducted into the Hall of Fame in 1983, the second year of elections.

Virginia is a traditional quiltmaker in most regards. "I haven't done machine-piecing, nor have I done anything other than hand-quilting," she says. "A lot of people do machine-quilting, but I don't particularly like it. I just feel it's not the real thing. So I don't do it." But quiltmakers are generous in their assessments and tolerant of other methods, and Virginia quickly adds, "Although some [machine-quilted quilts] look very beautiful. Everyone has their own choice of what they like to do."

Virginia's own method of quilting is somewhat unusual. "I lap quilt," she explains. "I don't use a frame. Just on my lap. I baste every two inches. Quite a job. It takes me quite awhile to do it. I spread it way out on the floor and I baste every two inches so that it's tightly held together. There's no chance of it getting puckered or slipped. And then I start in the middle and I lap quilt. It's not as easy, but I like it better."

Virginia works on a frame only when she attends a Patchworkers quilting. And it is the fellowship now, more than the quilting itself, which continues to draw her to the meetings. As they quilt together around the frame, the women in the guild share more than skills and knowledge. They share themselves, their lives, their joys and sorrows. In October of 1993, Virginia Roberts joined her fellow Patchworkers at one member's home to finish a quilt that member could not complete because of a disabling injury. It was a raw cold day, the start of winter in the Catskill high peaks. Virginia wasn't feeling well herself that day, but it would have been unthinkable to her not to answer the call. The day before, Virginia Roberts had quietly celebrated her eighty-seventh birthday.

Vivian Ruoff (b. 1920)

THE 50" BY 70" BED QUILT, "GONE BUT NOT FORGOTTEN," WAS HAND-APPLIQUED, EMBROIDERED AND HAND-QUILTED BY VIVIAN IN 1994 ENTIRELY FROM DEPRESSION-ERA FABRICS SHE COLLECTED OVER THE YEARS, INCLUDING AUTHENTIC FEEDSACKS FOR THE BACKING.

"At one time I think quilting really took over my life," Vivian Ruoff announced. Considering that in less than twenty years of quiltmaking Vivian had made seventy-five quilts, each of them entirely handmade, one could almost accuse Vivian of understatement. Vivian uses a sewing machine only for applying a border or for sewing blocks together. The tops are all hand-pieced or hand-appliqued, and each one of those seventy-five quilts was hand-quilted. "I used to turn them out like crazy, but I've slowed down," she says.

One of the reasons Vivian has "slowed down" is the competition from overseas. American quiltmakers nationwide have been hurt by the importation of inexpensive quilts from the Orient, and Vivian Ruoff, like most American quiltmakers, proudly refuses to compete. Even though "the Chinese quilts have changed the price range, we've refused to come down in the price of ours. If people want to buy them, okay," she says. The resentment goes deeper than economics, however. As Vivian declares, quiltmaking is "an American thing. We feel it belongs to us."

Vivian Ruoff has presented a quilt to each of her five children and eight grandchildren. The rest, aside from a couple of favorites she has kept for her own home, were sold: "They're all over the United States," she says. Before Vivian "slowed down," quiltmaking was a cottage industry for her. Many of her quilts were commissioned, created to a customer's exact specifications. But she found with time that quiltmaking-for-hire eroded her joy in the art. "It got too commercial," she says. "I didn't care for it anymore that way. It was no longer pleasure; it was business."

Vivian Ruoff was born in 1920 in the Greene County community of East Jewett, where she has continued to live for the last seventy-three years. Her ancestors were among the first to settle on the mountaintop. Six generations ago they carved out farms and harvested timber, but little remains in family possession today of the vast tracts of land they originally owned. Vivian reminisced about her grandfather, who held four thousand acres and operated a sawmill in the 1890s on land encircling today's Colgate Lake, now administered by New York State as part of the Catskill Park's Forest Preserve. "He wanted to go west and look for gold. He sold all the property for $1.00 an acre to Colgate. He paid him in gold. He had a little cigar box. They packed up everything and got on the train and went to Washington State."

But Vivian's parents stayed behind to raise a family and carve their own niche in the ever-difficult economy of the Catskills. Vivian recalls growing up during the Depression: "We didn't feel that much up here in the mountains because things didn't change that much for us. My father had a farm. We had everything we wanted." Mountaintop farm families were used to being self-sufficient, to making-do or doing without. The collapse of the macro-economy meant little to them because they were little involved with the economy. The nearby, affluent, private summer communities provided the opportunity to earn money to buy the few things that they could not make or raise themselves. As Vivian recalls, "Almost all of East Jewett worked for them," including Vivian's mother, who worked as a housekeeper during the summers for the actress Maude Adams at her estate in Onteora Park.

They survived and endured. But with farmwork and summer employment, Vivian's mother did not have the time to teach her daughter all of the finer points of sewing. When Vivian was twelve, her mother taught her to crochet, but Vivian's mother was not a quiltmaker. And according to Vivian, there was very little quiltmaking in all of East Jewett at that time, although she does recall once seeing a quilt on a frame at the East Jewett Methodist Church. There were quilts on the beds, but Vivian has no idea who made them. She does recall innocently sabotaging them, however: "I remember when I was a little kid and I was sick with some disease or something, I was in bed and I remember the little tufts–they tied quilts instead of quilting them, you know–I remember laying there and picking all those knots out, and my mother was furious with me!"

Vivian Ruoff had no experience in quiltmaking when, in 1973, together with her cousin and lifelong best friend, Doris Brooks, she founded the Patchworkers quilting guild. The motivation was to get "a woman's group together to just have fun and do things," she says. Quiltmaking, at first, was just the excuse. Doris Brooks and Vivian took informal lessons from Ruth Northrup, a neighbor who was an experienced quiltmaker. They began to meet Wednesday evenings with four or five other women from the East Jewett area. "Stitch and Bitch," as Vivian's husband referred to the Patchworkers, persevered and grew. In 1993, when the Patchworkers celebrated their 20th anniversary, the guild had grown to more than twenty-five members, including three inductees in the Hall of Fame. Two former members have also been inducted. "We've become a very close group," Vivian said. "It's better than a psychiatrist."

In addition to working with the newly-formed Patchworkers on their quilt projects—an activity she would participate in for over twenty years—Vivian began her own first quilt in 1973. It was a pieced eight-point star pattern, an ambitious choice for a beginner. She also soon began what would turn out to be a very fruitful partnership with Doris Brooks, as the two collaborated on a series of pictorial quilts. Brooks, an accomplished artist, would plan and draft the scenes for the various blocks on paper, and Vivian Ruoff would do the needlework, translating the drawings into paintings in fabric. Their first collaboration was a bicentennial quilt which is now in the collection of the Fenimore House Museum in Cooperstown. The translation from paper to fabric was not always a smooth one, as Vivian recalls: "She [Doris Brooks] used to hand me these patterns all drawn up. They looked beautiful on paper, but when you go to put them on material, that's another story. She did one block for me that was of the Twin Peaks [Round Top and High Peak, above Kaaterskill Clove] up by Onteora Church, that scene. And she had fog going over the mountains. And I said, 'Doris, how do I make fog!'" Vivian worked it out, however, and the finished quilt, entitled "Flora and Fauna of the Catskills," is a stunning tribute to the beauty of the Catskills and the cooperation of two talented artists. "Flora and Fauna of the Catskills" would have been a welcome addition to any museum but, unfortunately, Brooks and Ruoff sold that quilt to a private party in New York City. "After you sell something like that, you wish you hadn't," Vivian admits. However, "I felt that way about every quilt I ever sold," she adds.

Over the years, Vivian Ruoff became a leading proponent of quilt-making in the Catskills. She was one of the founding members of the Catskill Mountain Quilters Hall of Fame in 1982. She has taught quilt-making to many others through classes held in her own home and at the Home Extension in the village of Cairo. And she has stayed with the Patchworkers, for twenty years sharing her skills with new members and novices.

Vivian once made quilts at a frenetic pace to supplement her income. Now, her perspective has changed: "I want to leave something behind that people remember me by," she says. Her current passion is for Depression-era quilts, perhaps spurred by childhood memories of lying in bed more than sixty years ago untying that old quilt. She is working on her own "Depression quilt," using authentic period fabric for the top and feed sacks for the backing. Vivian notes how the times have changed: "They cost about ten bucks apiece now, those feed sacks. What the women in those days would think about that!"

Vivian Ruoff, now in her seventies, makes quilts solely for her own pleasure, at her own pace. "Nowadays," she scoffs, "It's hurry, hurry, hurry. Quilt-in-a-day, that always gets me. I always say, 'What's the rush? Take your time.'" As though in answer to any critic of American quiltmakers who might wonder why a handmade American quilt commands the price it does, Vivian points to a picture of her latest quilt, saying, "I quilted all winter on that." But Vivian's motive for quilt-making has transcended profit-seeking. As she eloquently stated, "I think it's pretty good therapy, quilting is. You sit down, and it's kind of like you have a rhythm, almost, like music."

Theresa Scheetz (b. 1946)

THERESA IN 1990. COLLECTION OF THE CATSKILL MOUNTAIN QUILTERS HALL OF FAME.

Theresa Scheetz (nee Valerio) moved to Fresno, Ohio, in 1990 after a twenty-year sojourn in the town of Lexington, Greene County. When she first arrived in the Catskills, Theresa knew almost nothing about quiltmaking. By the time she left, however, she had gained the skill and knowledge necessary to become a full-time professional quilt-maker, thus supplementing the income from the farm she and her husband own and operate. "I work at Gramma Fannie's Quilt Barn as quilt piecer and pattern designer," Theresa wrote in 1993. "I piece about two large quilts and ten wall hangings a month, and quilt about five of those wall quilts a year."

Theresa was born in Brooklyn in 1946. When she was ten years old, her family moved to Massapequa Park, Long Island, where she remained for the next 14 years. "If I still lived in New York City," Theresa said, "I might not have become a quilter. No one used or made quilts, or even knew anything about quilts [in NYC] in the 1960s." Theresa became an able seamstress however, having learned to sew at age five, and she had tried her hand at many, many crafts, acquiring along the way an eye for color and design which would later propel her into a career in the heady world of fashion design in Manhattan. She had always admired antique quilts and, in 1969, after having tried just about every other art and craft that exists, she made her first quilt, "Star Shadow." Theresa admits making "all the mistakes I possibly could," but she had discovered the art form that brought together her most consuming interests and pleasures, combining "all the elements of art and design with the physical satisfaction of working with a needle and fabric in your hand," she says.

The next year, Theresa moved to Lexington in the northern Catskills where, had she known to whom to turn, she could have found expert help with her quiltmaking. But Theresa was a newcomer, and quiltmaking in the Catskills at that time was largely the work of a few scattered individuals and church organizations—there were no guilds, nor quilt shows. And, as Theresa says, "There were no instructional books available, so I 'fudged' everything."

But she pressed on alone, making four more quilt tops during the next nine years "by trial and error," as she says. Soon, however, help was more readily available. Quiltmaking guilds began to sprout up everywhere, including the Patchworkers of nearby East Jewett, begun in 1973 by Doris Brooks and Vivian Ruoff. Theresa attended one of Doris Brooks's quiltmaking classes in 1979, "and from then on, I was hooked," she writes.

Thus began, for Theresa, an eleven-year period of frenetic activity in the burgeoning world of Catskill Mountains quiltmaking. She was in the right place at the right time, and she threw herself into the activities with an enthusiasm that few can match. "I joined the Patchworkers in 1980," Theresa writes, "Wiltwyck in 1981, SCRIDS in 1988, and was right there from the beginning of the Catskill Mountain Quilters Hall of Fame."

Theresa's already considerable artistic talents took root in this fertile ground, and she quickly went from novice student to expert quiltmaker, and became a leader within the quiltmaking community. In fact, Betty Verhoeven, co-president of the Hall of Fame in 1993, stated that were it not for Theresa's stewardship as president for four years, with the energy she committed to her post, the Hall of Fame might not have survived until today.

By 1983, Theresa was teaching quiltmaking, first in local fabric shops and guild meetings, and later in private lessons and at "The Quilter's Retreat" in Warwick, Orange County. Her own work began to gain wider recognition, garnering ribbons and awards at quilt shows throughout the Catskills, some of her works appearing in national quilt magazines. She became especially well-known for the fineness of her miniature quilts and wall-hangings, and her past experience in fashion design led naturally to experiments in patchworked and quilted clothing.

Theresa is an incessant experimenter. The same inquiring spirit which led her to try dozens of crafts before she found full expression for her talents in quiltmaking also drives her to try different techniques within the medium. "Most of my quilts are traditional, with lots of innovations," Theresa says. "I love re-designing old patterns." Even her very first quilt, "Star Shadow," was "a combination of the 'LeMoyne Star,' 'Basket Weave' and 'Spool Blocks,'" she writes.

Each quilted work became an adventure. Theresa added applique to her repertoire, followed by reverse applique, three-dimensional applique, tie-dying, and dyed color gradations. She replicated a turn-of-the-century "crazy quilt," complete with fancy embroidery. For her quilted clothing, she began to use beaded quilting. Even the "Mariner's Compass," her "all-time favorite quilt pattern," became innovative in her hands; Theresa developed a fast-piecing method for this most demanding and precise of traditional patterns.

She experimented with different fabrics as well, employing not only the traditional 100% cotton, but including also silks, blends, velvets, lace, wool and lamé "for special effects," she writes. And she likes to design her own quilting patterns, rather than relying on commercial patterns and stencils.

When Theresa married and moved to Ohio's Amish country in 1990, it might have seemed like a quilter's dream come true. She and her husband bought a farm, and Theresa was soon hired at the Quilt Barn where she could supplement the family income by working all day at the art she loves. But commissioned work can be constricting for an artist who is accustomed to giving free expression to her ideas. "The work I do for the shop is all custom orders to color and pattern specifications," she writes, "so there is little room for originality." Art becomes reduced to a trade under such circumstances; the artist becomes an artisan.

"The Amish enjoy quiltmaking and take it very seriously," Theresa says, "but it has become a business for them." She described in detail the progress of a "typical" commissioned Amish quilt:

> The typical tourist customer buys or orders a quilt to perfectly coordinate with the pink flowers in the wallpaper, or dusty blue in the wall-to-wall carpeting in their bedrooms. The Amish delight in making these beautiful pastel calico quilts, as they cannot use these fabrics for their own quilts .... One Amish woman will piece the top, then send it to another to mark the quilt designs, and on to another older woman relative to quilt, and binding to another, till it comes back to be sold at a consignment shop, or in their own home. A real cottage industry.

Although Ohio Amish quiltmaking may resemble a factory assembly line, Theresa adds, "Their workmanship is wonderful, and the sale price does not begin to cover the hours at the treadle sewing machine and the quilt frame under gaslight." However, she continues, "Somehow I get the feeling, after talking with these Amish quilters, with all the deadlines and orders, they do not feel the excitement that a guild member gets when starting a new quilt." It is the age-old conflict between art and the marketplace, between the artist and the patron, a situation requiring compromise.

Theresa, with her love of self-expression and experiment, looks back with nostalgia to her time in the Catskills:

> *Now that I have lived in the heart of Ohio's Amish country for three years, I see many differences in regional quilting, not so much in the methods used or the stitches, patterns and colors, but in the attitudes of the quilters. In* [upstate] *New York, we all quilted for the joy of creating a thing of beauty. The groups we belonged to nourished, inspired and encouraged that creativity .... The Catskills are full of wonderful quilts and quilters.* [Theresa Valerio Scheetz, 1993]

Betty Verhoeven (b. 1930)

THE 70" BY 70" BED QUILT, "D-VINE HEARTS," WAS HAND-APPLIQUED AND HAND-QUILTED BY BETTY FROM AN ORIGINAL DESIGN BY HER DAUGHTER, JOHANNA. IT WAS COMPLETED IN 1992.

One of the blue ribbon quilts entered in the 1993 Calico Geese Quilt Show depicts Betty Verhoeven's journey through life with the succinctness and symbolism, and the understated beauty, of great poetry. Up close, it appears to be an abstract work, an artful jumble of small squares of colored cloth neatly sewn in rows. A few steps back and a unifying pattern starts to appear, with bars of different colors, small stars, and a stylized maple leaf in the center. Starting from the top left corner, the Dutch flag gradually dissolves into the Canadian flag in the middle, which in turn, row by row, piece by piece, transforms into the American flag in the bottom right corner. The transitions are as smooth and seamless as the metamorphoses in M. C. Escher drawings. Designed with the aid of her oldest daughter, Johanna, and flawlessly executed entirely by Betty's own hands, it is a tour de force, representing not only the three flags that fly over lands in which she has made her home, but graphically illustrating how those uprootings and relocations, the different segments and landmarks of her past, form the harmony of a rich and varied life.

Betty was born in the little village of Diessen, Holland, in 1930. Her childhood was idyllic enough, although her teen years would be marred by the uncertainty, fear and wartime shortages of life under German occupation. She was educated in a private finishing school where a part of the curriculum was devoted to handcrafts and needle work. As a child, Betty hated sewing and failed her needlework courses, but she was expected to contribute to the family's material needs, regardless of her inclinations. "You could never sit down at night and do nothing, or play cards like the boys would do," she recalls. "Your hands had to always be busy. It needed to be done. It was wartime. My mother was always sewing. Knitting and crocheting was done because socks needed to be knitted and sweaters to be done." Sundays became her favorite day of the week because then, "you were allowed to work on your finer pieces," she adds. "Mostly, embroidery was your fine work."

Although she still hated to sew, Betty started making all of her own clothes by her early teens, out of necessity. She had no way of foreseeing it then, but for the next fifty years she would continue to make clothes for herself and her family, and would eventually find a creative outlet and supplemental income by home-producing Victorian and patchwork clothing–everything from wedding dresses and Victorian Christmas stockings to backpacks, hats and winter coats. The little girl who failed sewing in school would become an innovative designer and inspired seamstress.

After the war, Betty married and her travels soon began. She and her husband packed their belongings in steamer trunks and set sail for Canada in 1954. Like generations of New World immigrants before them–commercial air travel was still in its pioneering days–they said goodbye to their families with little hope of ever seeing them again.

Canada was good to the Verhoevens. They stayed for eleven years, worked hard, saved and eventually bought their own farm. But it was not an easy life, especially at first, and Betty's talents helped keep the family clothed. Christmas presents were rarely purchased–Betty would hand-sew winter coats, dresses or shirts, or make stuffed animals for her children.

By 1965, the Verhoevens were ready to move on. Betty's husband, Jack, had his sights set on Virginia, but a job offer landed them in East Jewett, Greene County, on a storybook farm in a small fertile valley surrounded by the high peaks of the Catskills. The Verhoevens were more prosperous now and Betty had more time to pursue creative interests. She began to make items to sell at craft shows. At first she specialized in leather goods–pocketbooks, vests and jackets–all done in a "patchwork style." With the boom in denim clothing in the 1960s and early 1970s, she moved on to patchwork denim articles. Then she spied a Victorian pillow at one show, and she threw her energies into producing Victorian clothing and accessories in muslin and lace.

Finally, in 1975, Betty was introduced to quiltmaking by one of her neighbors, Florence DeLong, whom the whole family had begun to call "Grandma." Florence belonged to a quilting society at the East Jewett Methodist Church, and she taught quiltmaking in her home to the few who were interested in learning at that time. She started Betty on a "Cathedral Windows" coverlet. It was the first of nearly 100 coverlets, quilts and wall-hangings Betty would produce in the next 19 years.

That first "Cathedral Windows" took two years for Betty to finish. "I used all my children's clothing in it," she says. Later, Betty sold it for $500, a transaction she still regrets. "I let it go, and that's kind of a shame that I did that," she explains. "I didn't really need the money. You do it because you feel kind of excited when you sell something. But on the other hand, you're giving something away that you worked so hard on."

With Betty's interest in fabric, it is surprising that she did not become involved in quiltmaking sooner. But back in Holland, as she explains, "I never saw anybody work on quilts. We slept under quilted quilts. They were wholecloth pieces. Where they came from, I don't know." Her family still has some of those quilts, from the 1930s or earlier, and on a recent trip home Betty inspected them closely. The tops were pieced together from one fabric, a woolen blanket was inserted for the batting, and the three layers were machine-quilted.

Similarly, during her eleven years in Canada, Betty never met a quiltmaker, and she doesn't recall ever seeing patchwork quilts. But the Catskills in 1975 were beginning to bloom with quilts, and quiltmaking guilds were starting to form. The first such guild, the Patchworkers of East Jewett, had already been in existence for three years, and Betty joined them in 1978. As she immersed herself in quiltmaking, Betty became more and more involved in quiltmaking organizations. She joined Wiltwyck in 1980, SCRIDS in 1990, and served as president of the Catskill Mountain Quilters Hall of Fame from 1989 to 1994.

She also began to amass prize ribbons—almost thirty in all by 1994—for her quilted art, including first prize in two national quilt block contests and a blue ribbon at the 1983 New York State Fair. She shared her skills and knowledge by teaching quiltmaking techniques in guild and craft shop seminars, at the Cooperative Extension, in elementary schools and in her own home.

Betty Verhoeven, like many quiltmakers in the Catskills today, mixes traditional elements with innovation in the creation of her art. "When I began quilting, I loved stars," she states. "Now I love a wide range of patterns. I like to work with traditional patterns, but change enough of the design so it becomes my own." In recent years, more and more of the patterns she uses are original designs, but Betty discussed the difficulty of creating something truly new within such an ancient and universal tradition: "You think you see something different, and it's been done—unless you do very abstract work." It is a dilemma faced by twentieth-century artists in every medium.

Betty prefers applique over piecing, and she considers her appliqued quilts her best work. Sometimes she incorporates trapunto to add a three-dimensional effect. Among her blue ribbon works are a series of quilted wall-hangings with trapunto inspired by old *Vogue* magazine covers. They were executed in "white on white" and the result is like bas-relief sculpture.

For her own quilts, Betty often uses the "quilt-as-you-go" method, employing a lap hoop. Her active guild participation, however, means many hours around a large frame—but that, too, has its rewards. "I like to sit around a big quilt frame with a bunch of women," Betty says. "I like that togetherness a lot."

For the past nineteen years, quiltmaking has consumed much of Betty's time and has become her primary form of creative expression, but her other arts and talents have not lain idle. She has won awards for her photography, and "The Dutch Touch," Betty's home-based outlet for her original clothing designs, continues to supplement her income. Victorian dresses hang side-by-side with patchwork vests. "I cannot do just one thing," she states. "I need different outlets for my energy."

But, as she quickly adds, "Quilters stay quilters." In the spring of 1994, Betty had just finished what she called her "Dutch Quilt." She had brought all of the fabrics back from Holland, and the pattern was from an antique Dutch quilt she had seen—a combination of "Snowball" and "Eight-Pointed Star." It is the latest in an ambitious project to make a quilt for each of her relatives still in Holland, where patchwork quiltmaking, influenced by the American renaissance, has become very popular again for the first time in generations. "They call it 'the American Quilting,'" Betty explained.

Like a sculptor seeing a form take shape out of a block of marble, or a composer hearing harmony form from the infinite possibilities lying dormant in an untouched keyboard, Betty Verhoeven spoke of the magic of creating art out of fabric: "You see a pattern come alive ... You start with scraps and then you see something come alive under your hands."

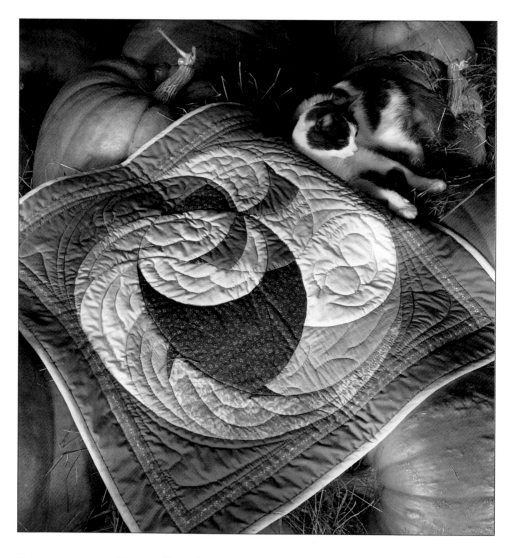

"SKATER IN THE ROUND" BY CONNIE STANGEL. THIS 30" BY 30" WALL-HANG-ING WAS HAND-PIECED AND HAND-QUILTED BY CONNIE IN 1989, FROM A PAT-TERN BY JEAN JOHNSON.

CHAPTER 7

Schoharie County

It is not so much the mountains in Schoharie County that take your breath away, it is the valley. Driving south on Route 145 from Cobleskill, the road clinging to the steep slope of a hill, the view opens up of a deep wide valley with sharply ascending hills on either side. It looks so rich and full of promise, it is no wonder that colonials staked their lives to homestead there in the years just prior to the Revolution when the Schoharie Valley was a true frontier.

Those risks increased with the war years. A marauding force of Tories and Iroquois invaded the valley and, although turned away by a small garrison at today's Old Stone Fort Museum, they burned houses and barns and destroyed crops, forcing an evacuation of the more isolated and vulnerable outposts. In so doing, they accomplished the more important goal of instilling terror in the population and tying up scarce colonial troops.

But that was a long time ago, and the English are once again welcome in Schoharie, provided they spend well at the roadside farmstands and buy souvenirs at Howe Caverns. Even the Iroquois now have their own museum, just off I-88, proving once again that when you win, it's easy to be gracious.

Schoharie has its share of rock-strewn hillside dairy farms, but the valley itself is rich and fertile. At one time, it was one of the leading producers of hops for a thirsty young nation; now it is a supplier of vegetables and fruits to the nearby Capital District.

Just north of Schoharie the foothills of the Adirondacks begin to rise; to the south the high peaks of the Catskills lie in the distance. Wedged in between, Schoharie was one of the first gateways to the west in the late eighteenth and early nineteenth centuries, and old inns and trading posts still dot the highways, side-by-side with convenience stores and diners catering to more modern needs.

I-88 has brought a new cosmopolitanism to this outlying Catskill Mountains county, connecting it closely to Schenectady with mutual ties—an easy commute for county natives in search of employment; a nearby haven for urbanites in search of a country home. Although the recent decline in the fortunes of that city's General Electric-based economy threatens those ties, for Schoharie County quiltmakers access to Schenectady still means one very important thing—access to Q.U.I.L.T.S, one of the largest guilds in upstate New York.

Christine Polak (b. 1945)

The 103" by 103" bed quilt, "North Carolina Lily," was machine-pieced and hand-quilted by Chris as a wedding gift for her brother John and his wife Ann, who live in North Carolina. It was completed in 1992. Chris wrote: "The layout came from a picture I saw, and then I added the vines."

For Chris Polak, quiltmaking is a manifestation of happiness. If that inner wellspring of peace and contentment, for any reason, ceases to flow to the surface, she cannot focus her mind on the creation of beautiful objects. "In the past twelve years," Chris stated in 1993, "I've made at least 35 full-size quilts, about 30 wall-hangings, about 25 miniature quilts, and helped with 9 raffle quilts." They must have been happy years.

Chris was born in Middleburgh in 1945, and traces her ancestry back four generations in Schoharie County. Her ancestors ran dairy farms and grew hops (for which the Schoharie Valley was once renowned), but her father broke with his family's agricultural tradition when he moved from Richmondville to Middleburgh to open a funeral parlor.

Chris's mother, though not a quiltmaker, had a formative influence on Chris's later avocation by exposing her at an early age to a wide range of sewing skills. "My mother sewed everything," Chris recalls, "clothes, draperies, stuffed animals. She could even make tailored suits," Chris adds, as well as write children's books (two were published), and she studied painting.

Today, that combination of sewing ability and artistic inclination would almost certainly find expression in quiltmaking, but in the 1940s and 1950s quilts were out of vogue. "We had them on our beds," Chris recalls. "And I can distinctly remember—because we laugh about it now—they had what they called 'counterpanes' that they put between the mattress and the springs. And I know they were between our beds on the springs." Those quilts, or "counterpanes," were held in such low esteem that their final resting place was completely out of sight, their sole purpose to protect the mattress. "Inevitably they had rust spots on them," Chris adds.

Chris assumes that those quilts on the beds and the counterpanes underneath were made by her Richmondville grandmother, but she cannot be sure. Her grandmother did make many quilts, some of which have survived the years of use (and abuse) to be preserved and passed down in the family, but her grandmother died when Chris was very young, so Chris missed the opportunity to witness the actual quiltmaking.

Chris made her own first quilts in the late 1960s and early 1970s, during her first marriage. "I didn't need them," she states. "I just liked to sew." Completely untutored, really without a clue as to how to proceed, Chris admits that those first quilts were "horrible ugly things I'm sure—doubleknits mixed in with cottons." The designs were simple. Chris would often just "take squares of fabric and sew them together," and then, "I would just tie them," she adds. "There was so little on quilting back then, just what you might see in a magazine."

Today, Chris is recognized as one of the region's most expert quiltmakers, so she likes to take samples of her early work, warts and all, to guild meetings to motivate and encourage beginning quilters. "People, for some reason, think you start at the top," Chris explains. "They don't know that you made all those mistakes."

After those tentative beginnings, Chris abandoned quiltmaking until the early 1980s. Raising three small children, while having to assume the burden of the chores around the farm where she then lived, left her with little time to spare. They were hard years, and not the happiest for Chris; the quiltmaking muse was silent, her hands were still.

By the early 1980s, Chris's situation had changed and improved, and with the children older and in school, she suddenly found that she had spare time again. The pivotal moment came in 1982 when Chris met Arlene Vrooman ("the best quilter I know," Chris says) at a craft show in the nearby village of Summit. Recalling her own, admittedly clumsy, attempts at quiltmaking ten years previously, Chris was moved and impressed by the artistry displayed by Arlene and others at the show.

Chris signed up for a six to eight-week adult education course in quiltmaking, taught by Arlene. "It was then that I really got the bug, big time," she says. Arlene Vrooman is known as an expert and patient—but rigorous—instructor, and Chris remembers, "I spent more time with a seam-ripper in my hand, because she wanted it to be perfect." But "she put me on the right track," Chris adds.

The instruction rounded out what she had been able to learn on her own and, combined with her sewing skills and a lifetime occupied with crafts and handwork, Chris was ready to make quilts again—real quilts this time, not tied off as comforters. She produced nearly 100 quilted works in the next dozen years.

Chris works almost every day on quiltmaking. "I generally have two or three quilts going at the same time," she says. She carefully drafts the design on graph paper, finding inspiration in quilting magazines or by exchanging ideas with other quilters. Although she hand-quilts each work, which can take up to six months depending upon the size of the work and the quilting patterns, Chris pieces by machine. "They hold together better, it's faster, and you can be as accurate on the machine as you can by hand," she says. And although she owns a large floor frame, she prefers the comfort of quilting with a lap hoop, the warm folds of fabric enveloping her as she works.

Chris Polak doesn't have a favorite pattern, although she has made many "Star" variations. She likes to try different designs, always experimenting a little. While she adamantly insists her work is not "original," every quilt she has made has her own imprint on it, some slight variation, and she admits that she doesn't always "march to the same tune." She now employs both piecing and applique, but applique is a more recently-acquired skill. "I had to force myself to learn, because it's hard." Then she adds, laughing, "Arlene made me!"

"You never stop learning," Chris says. She has amassed a substantial library of books on quiltmaking, subscribes to four magazines devoted to the art and she attends three different guilds, including the Schoharie Valley Piecemakers of which she was a founding member.

All of this activity does not stem from an idle life of leisure; Chris Polak is a working woman who manages a greenhouse. But she is a dedicated and determined artist who somehow finds the time to pursue, and continually refine, her art. Her technique and craftsmanship produce quilted art as finely-wrought and meticulously constructed as any to be found–the happy result of her native determination, coupled with the exacting standards instilled in her by Arlene Vrooman.

Like any true artist in any medium, Chris's spirit rebels against "hack" work. She can only make a quilt that she wants to make. "I've made quilts for other people," she says, "and learned the hard way never to make a quilt just for the money. She [one patron] wanted a design that I hated, and they were colors that I hated. I couldn't force myself to work on it." Chris ended up paying someone else to finish that quilt.

Again like any true artist in any medium, Chris Polak will not compromise: "I really don't make quilts for other people's satisfaction, but I do want it to be as right as I can make it for myself. That's just the way it is. I'm not happy slapping something together. Can't do it. And I *won't* do it."[Chris Polak, 1993]

Viola Scranton (b. 1910)

THE 72" BY 78" BED QUILT, "SCRAPAHOLIC NINE-PATCH," WAS HAND-APPLIQUED AND HAND-QUILTED BY VIOLA BETWEEN MAY AND AUGUST, 1991. VIOLA WROTE OF THIS QUILT: "THE SCRAPAHOLIC NINE-PATCH DESIGN WAS TAUGHT IN A CLASS BY GLORIA HARTLEY FROM MAHOPAC, NEW YORK. NINE 9" SQUARES OF FABRIC WERE STACKED, CUT AT RANDOM, AND THEN ASSEMBLED SO EACH FABRIC WOULD BE PLACED AT A DIFFERENT POSITION AND EMBROIDERED TO A SOLID COLOR. I CHOSE A BLACK BACKGROUND AS IT MADE EACH BLOCK STAND OUT AND THE LOOK IS 'ANTIQUE-ISH.'"

*W*hen Viola Scranton retired from her career as a high school science teacher in 1970, one of her first projects was to set up her quilting frame and complete a quilt she had begun in the 1930s. She took up, literally, where she had left off, the thirty-five-year hiatus having no effect whatsoever. By 1993 Viola had completed 50 to 60 hand-quilted items, from bed quilts to place mats, pillows, pillow shams and wall-hangings, and she had been instrumental in reviving the art of quilt-making in Schoharie County.

Viola Scranton's journey began in Sweden, where she was born in 1910. Her parents emigrated to America when Viola was very young and, after a brief sojourn in New York City, the family moved to a farm near Blenheim Hill in Delaware County when Viola was five. As income from the farm was not enough to support the family, Viola's father was forced to work "off the farm," Viola said, so most of the farmwork fell upon Viola's mother and the children. Consequently, Viola's mother, burdened with heavy farm work, a family to raise and a home to maintain, never had time to spare to teach sewing to her daughters–an ironic beginning for Viola Scranton and Astrid Ormiston, the only two sisters to be inducted into the Catskill Mountain Quilters Hall of Fame.

Viola's only education in sewing, therefore, was gleaned from classes at school and 4-H meetings. It was enough, however, to provide her with the basic skills to build on when the opportunity to use them would arise. And the family's hard work paid off for Viola. She was able to get her teaching degree and launch her own career. Her first teaching position began in 1932 in Rose's Brook, a small community in Delaware County. It was not far from Blenheim Hill, but in the early 1920s it was not an easy commute, so Viola boarded with a family near the school–a common practice for young school teachers in those days. The woman Viola boarded with was a quiltmaker. Viola watched and studied her work and began making quilts herself, "to pass the time," she said.

She continued piecing tops and quilting after she married, moved to the village of Schoharie and began to raise her own family. In fact, one of her sons, while in the military, traveled all over the United States and overseas with one of Viola's quilts tucked into his duffel bag. But after her children reached school age, Viola resumed her teaching career. With the twin demands of a family and a career to absorb her time, the quilting frame was packed away until her retirement in 1970.

Always a very active woman, Viola, after her retirement, channeled much of her energies into quiltmaking. She worked on her own for a few years and then discovered there was a growing interest in quiltmaking among her neighbors in the Schoharie Valley. She helped found the Schoharie Valley Piecemakers Quilt Guild, and she eventually joined a second guild. A third group meets informally in Viola's home from September to May. Viola has taught many other women to make quilts, "including home economics teachers," as she said with a smile.

Viola is a very traditional quiltmaker. Sometimes she pieces by machine, but all of her quilts are hand-quilted on a large frame. She favors traditional patterns, both pieced and appliqued. And she does not sell her work. What she hasn't given to her children and grandchildren adorns her own home, entering which is like walking into a museum. In addition to her own quilted works, which are displayed on every bed, table, chair and sofa, Viola has a fine collection of antique quilts.

One, passed down through generations of her husband's family, is a blue and white pieced "Star" pattern with a "Garden Maze" border, which may date from as early as the 1850s. Another quilt in her collection, photographed and catalogued by the Museum of American Folk Art, is a raffle quilt made by the Ladies Aid Society of the Reformed Church of Central Bridge. It consists of red and white squares embroidered with names, initials, birds, flowers and the date of completion, 1891. These quilts testify to a strong tradition of quiltmaking in Schoharie County's past, a tradition revived, renewed and more alive than ever in the 1990s because of the efforts and example of a few women like Viola Scranton.

Anna Marie Tucker (b. 1932)

The 70" by 80" bed quilt, "Not Just Another Log Cabin," produced from cotton remnants collected since the 1950s, was machine-pieced, hand-appliqued and hand-quilted by Anna Marie in 1988. This quilt appeared on the cover of *Traditional Quilter*.

"I've just been sewing forever," Anna Marie stated, with only slight exaggeration. She began to sew when she was two years old. "I watched my grandmother," she explained. "I would watch her, and I would go home and do it. I was making my clothes by the time I was eight." Sixty years later, as the owner and sole employee of The Quilt Barn in the hilltop hamlet of Summit, Schoharie County, Anna Marie spends every day with fabric, needles and thread. "Quilt shops come and go," she says. "It's not as romantic as you might imagine. I treat this like I would treat any other job going out to work. I come out here [to the shop] nine in the morning, and I'm out here until three or four in the afternoon." But Anna Marie is not quite as chained to the work table as that statement would lead you to believe; she has become an itinerant instructor, as well as an avid follower of the quilt show circuit, and one is almost as apt to find Anna Marie in Cape Cod, Vermont, Long Island—or even Alaska or Japan—as in Summit, which is why The Quilt Barn's advertised hours are "By Chance or Appointment."

Anna Marie still has a slight accent which betrays her Brooklyn upbringing. She was born near Ebbets Field in 1932, and she still follows baseball on television. (Like most Brooklynites, however, her loyalties are no longer with the Dodgers.) Quilting and baseball may seem an odd combination of pastimes, but Anna Marie has discovered a nationwide baseball/quilting club which corresponds and shares patterns and stats through computer electronic mail. Quiltmaking today just isn't what it used to be.

Anna Marie's childhood interest in sewing continued unabated through her teen years. She studied design and drafting in high school and put those skills to use as a clothing designer and dressmaking instructor when she graduated. In later years, in a reversal of the usual pattern, Anna Marie's mother attended one of her classes and learned from her daughter how to sew and make clothes.

With her talents and her interest in design and drafting, it is natural that Anna Marie should eventually take up quiltmaking, but "We had no quilts in our family," she states. "I saw my first quilt in '59 at the Cookstown Fair and I said, 'Some day I'm going to make one.' And I had been collecting fabrics since I was a child. When I saw quilts, I said, 'Now I know what I'm going to do!'"

That resolution, however, was to remain unrealized for another thirteen years while Anna Marie continued to teach and design clothing. In 1972 she decided to attempt a "Grandmother's Flower Garden." Characteristically, she experimented and improvised: "At that time, there was only one book in the library, and it was on 'English Piecing.' I said, 'I am *not* cutting out 3,600 pieces of paper!' So I went home and I came up with what I call my 'un-English Method'–I used to call it the 'Brooklyn Method'–and it's the method I teach to this day. I just cut out one template and use it over and over and over. It has to be a flexible template so you can flip it out and use it. And when you're done, there's no basting to remove, either." Anna Marie estimates that her "un-English Method" for piecing cuts the time in half. Twenty-two years later, "Flower Garden" quilts remain a passion. "I always have a hexagon quilt in the works," she adds.

"Little by little, my classes switched to quilting," Anna Marie continues. Never one to avoid a challenge, she began to teach quiltmaking when her own first quilt was only half-completed. "It was just a matter of keeping one step ahead of the class every week," she says.

It was learn-as-you-go for teacher and students alike. Anna Marie recalls how she introduced an entire class of children to the magic of quiltmaking. At the end of one day, Anna Marie retrieved some fabric that one of the girls in the class had discarded in the wastebasket. That night, Anna Marie made a "Flower" from the remnants and showed it to the girl the next day. "Suddenly every child in the class wanted to be in the quilt," Anna Marie says. So she made "Flowers" from the fabrics each child had leftover, including "wools, polyesters, flannels, Hawaiian prints, velveteens, corduroy. I didn't know there were rules and regulations," she adds.

Her classes became so popular that Anna Marie had to add an extension to her house to accommodate them. Five days a week, Anna Marie taught two or three classes a day. "When I left Long Island, my waiting list to get into classes was over 200," she says. "They used to say, 'You have to wait for someone to die to get into her class.'"

Sadly, trouble was brewing. Anna Marie's husband became sick in 1976 and had to leave his job, making Anna Marie the principal breadwinner in the family. Then, one of her neighbors reported to the authorities that Anna Marie was operating a commercial enterprise in a community zoned strictly residential. "I went to church that Sunday," Anna Marie recalls, "and the sermon was 'Take Your Talents and Go,' so I came home and said, 'We're moving!'"

The blue mountains of the Catskills beckoned. In 1977, in the middle of a snowstorm, Anna Marie and her husband moved to Summit. "I had decided I was going to open a quilt shop," she recalls. "There really weren't quilt shops at that time—very few and far between." The Tuckers bought a small farm and immediately set about refurbishing the barn into a studio and classroom, and Anna Marie was soon back in business. She was amazed at her reception in Summit; people came from all over to attend her classes. Soon, she instituted all-day sessions because her students often had to drive long distances to attend. Children came as well, including boys, which surprised Anna Marie. She had anticipated that country boys would be solely interested in "Huckleberry Finn activities."

Because of the remoteness of the hamlet of Summit, Anna Marie also became a traveling instructor, her journeys gradually taking her further and further afield. Every year she teaches a series of quiltmaking retreats at Marie's Dream House, a small resort in the mountain valley of Westkill, Greene County. Students "come from all over," Anna Marie explains. "From Virginia, New Mexico, even Japan." The retreats last four days and three nights, and by the time the students have departed, they have designed and completed a quilt top.

Two of Anna Marie's most memorable teaching experiences came in Japan and Alaska. In Japan, she was invited to teach a class in her "un-English" method of piecing "Grandmother's Flower Garden," and she was also invited to attend Japanese guild meetings, which feature their own version of "show and tell." "I really had my eyes opened up when I looked at Japanese quilts," she explained. She was particularly fascinated by the way traditional American patterns become transmuted in the hands of Japanese quiltmakers:

You want to see "Log Cabin" quilts, you have to see Japanese quilts ... They're not inhibited by tradition because they don't know what our tradition is ... They're coming up with things that, when we look at them, we don't recognize them because the tradition of the color, or what's dark and what's light, changed.

Partly inspired by that experience, Anna Marie began her own experiments with traditional patterns, such as curved "Log Cabins," or landscaping a "Grandmother's Flower Garden" below a "Log Cabin" pattern on a quilt. She combines applique with piecing. Instead of appliqueing onto a white background, Anna Marie superimposes her appliqued work onto a "Log Cabin" or "Ohio Star," creating a marriage of two techniques for a very rich look. One would think the result would be an overly "busy" design, but the quilts are so artfully crafted that isolating the ground pattern becomes a surprising discovery.

Another eye-opener for Anna Marie was her trip to Alaska. "I went there to work with the Indians and Eskimos and homesteaders because they have such a terrible depression and drinking and drug problem because of the darkness," Anna Marie explained. "So I went in the winter to teach them quilting." Her sponsors were missionaries who thought the therapeutic effects of quiltmaking might help cure some of the widespread social problems. Anna Marie spent a few weeks traveling from village to village, house to house, sharing her quiltmaking skills. Her reception was warm and enthusiastic, and her students' color choices gave Anna Marie insight into color psychology. "I brought fabric along because we were working in a way-out-of-the-way place," she begins. Included was a bolt of bright yellow fabric from her shop in Summit, which became the hands-down favorite:

> And it dawned on me—they wanted the brightness, the sunshine. And I think that's where, with today's quilting, you have different areas with different colors, because they're more appropriate for the different areas where they are. Like in the southwest you find softer colors. I think we [in the northeast] want brighter colors, and I think it has to do with the climate.

Back in The Quilt Barn in Summit, Anna Marie puts her insights and experiences to work as she designs a new quilt, the latest of "hundreds, easily" which she has made. Not all of her experiments are successful, but she is creative enough to salvage some form of victory from any near-defeat. As she explains, "If you have a block you want to try out, and you find you don't like it, it goes into a potholder. And the potholders have put many loaves of bread on the table when nothing else came in."

Anna Marie greets with characteristic good humor the general public's ignorance of the time and effort that goes into her art. "People walk in and say, 'I'm going to a wedding on Saturday. Can you please make me a "Double Wedding Ring?"' And I say, 'Sure. I'd love to do that. It will be ready in one year.' They're so surprised, but I say, 'Well, as long as you wait a year you'll know if the marriage is going to hold up or not!'"

Commissions are welcomed, "but I prefer to teach them how to do it themselves," Anna Marie explains. "I think it's more rewarding to the individual. I don't think you can appreciate a quilt, or the money you pay for a quilt, until you've tried to do some quilting yourself." The rewards are greater for the teacher, as well. As Anna Marie continues, "I enjoy seeing what others can do when they're shown. It's nice when you teach a class and then get to see all the quilted items after. Or you go to a show and you see your designs repeated over and over, and other people's interpretations of your designs."

Anna Marie is actively involved in two quilt guilds and she is an honorary member of several others, periodically receiving their newsletters and monitoring their activities. Quiltmaking for Anna Marie is an art, a business, and a consuming passion around which her life revolves. You might find her at work at The Quilt Barn "by chance or appointment." Or you might find her at a quilt show or seminar wherever you are. For The Quilt Barn is merely home base and launching pad for one of the most active, gifted, knowledgeable and dedicated quiltmakers in the country.

Arlene Vrooman (b. 1928)

The 74" by 90" bed quilt, "A Tribute to My Mother," was designed, hand-appliqued, hand-pieced and hand-quilted by Arlene in 1989. Arlene and her mother graduated from the same music school—Academy of Holy Names, Albany—twenty-five years apart from each other. The design is of an open music book, with the bottom page representing a concert stage with two grand pianos. The hands, traced from Arlene's grandchildren, represent the students Arlene and her mother taught. Musical symbols and instruments are quilted throughout the entire work.

*J*ust on the outskirts of the historic village of Schoharie is a large, rambling, red brick farmhouse perched on a hill with a commanding view of the Schoharie Valley. The original part of the house is over 200 years old and was built to replace an older homestead burned to the ground by Joseph Brant's raiding party of Tories and Iroquois during their devastating sweep through the valley during the Revolution. Schoharie at that time was on the edge of the American frontier, the flashpoint of clashing cultures. Today it is a picturesque and peaceful little village filled with echoes of the past, and the red brick farmhouse, site of past carnage, is home to Arlene and Hank Vrooman, two of the most talented folk artists in the Catskills.

Arlene was born in Albany in 1928. She did not move to Schoharie until 1946, as the eighteen-year-old bride of Hank Vrooman, but her family's roots in Schoharie reach back a couple of generations. As a young girl and teenager in the 1930s and 1940s she spent many of her summers and Christmas vacations with her Schoharie Valley paternal grandparents, so the move in 1946 was like going home again.

Arlene was already a talented needleworker by that time, and she was certified as a piano teacher. The pressures of raising a family left her with no time to pursue a musical career, but her sewing skills helped the family survive. Looking back, in 1993, Arlene wrote, "I have sewed for 50 years out of necessity—making my own clothes while in high school, then for my seven children, and had a business in my home repairing and making clothes for many years." Years later, Arlene's sewing skills and longing for artistic expression would blend together, and she would create some of the most virtuoso and poetic quilted art in the Catskills.

Her initiation into the needlework arts came early. Both of her grandmothers were skilled and taught her sewing, embroidery, knitting and crochet before Arlene was ten. By age eleven, she could applique. So it is almost strange that Arlene did not also learn the quilter's art when she was young, especially as her paternal grandmother in Schoharie—whom Arlene visited every summer—was a quilter, and Arlene still has that grandmother's quilt patterns clipped from magazines in the 1930s. But perhaps we must remember that for many rural women of that era, quiltmaking was strictly a winter activity.

It wasn't until Arlene married and moved permanently to Schoharie that she was introduced to the art of quilting. At first, the quilts were strictly functional, "utilitarian quilts." Her landlady presented her with a tied baby quilt made back in 1912 from scraps of salvageable material from used aprons, shirts and pajamas. Then she showed Arlene how to make a quilt from used milk strainer squares—four by four-inch squares of flannel sold by the box to dairy farmers—a common method of straining milk until the 1950s. The used squares would be rinsed out and dyed (usually orange), then pieced together with alternating white squares to form a rudimentary pattern, and finally tied to a backing with a batting in between. They were "very warm," Arlene remembers, but "they had the old [cotton] batting in them, so after they were washed they got kind of lumpy."

Arlene continued to make tied quilts for home consumption through the 1950s and 1960s, but most of her time was given to raising her seven children, making clothes for the family and operating her home-based seamstress business. By the early 1970s, her children were older and Arlene found she had the time to turn her talents in another direction. Two friends, Laura Kane and Viola Scranton, introduced Arlene to "the quilting method," as she writes, and Arlene became an active participant in the Schoharie County bicentennial quilt.

Arlene's skills were in high demand during the bicentennial—she also made costumes for the county's parades and exhibits, which motivated her later to make more quilts. As Arlene explained, "They wore the long calico dresses, and I had this business of making clothes and repairing clothes, so I made a lot of those long dresses for everybody. And then you have those scraps, and now it's time to make quilts! And that's the way quiltmaking ought to be."

Thus began a new era in Arlene's life. She continued to make clothes, both for herself and for customers, but quiltmaking started to consume more and more of her time and energy. She joined the newly-formed Schoharie Valley Piecemaker's Quilt Guild and, later, Q.U.I.L.T.S. (Quilters United In Learning Together, Schenectady—a nearby 200-member urban organization). As one of the few experienced quilters in the Schoharie Valley in the mid- to late 1970s, Arlene became a quiltmaking instructor in high demand, sharing her knowledge in guild workshops, seminars in fabric stores, private lessons in her own home, and adult education classes in area schools. She demonstrated quiltmaking at arts councils and to area schoolchildren, and she became a judge of quilts at fairs and shows.

Quiltmaking and related arts became a cottage industry for Arlene, supplementing the money she still earns from making clothes. Quilted wall-hangings, pillows, table runners, clothing and potholders are churned out in quantity from Arlene's workshop, but the quality never varies. Arlene is famous throughout the region for her perfectionism and technical skill. She is a demanding instructor and critic, but she is equally stern in regard to her own work. If it isn't the best she can do, the stitches are ripped out and it is re-done until it passes judgment. Repairing antique quilts has become a specialty for Arlene. Collectors and dealers seek her out from as far away as New York City and beyond. The most frequent repair is replacing the old lumpy batting in tied quilts, or adding a backing to a crazy quilt throw. But sometimes the top needs repair as well, and Arlene's huge storeroom of remnants and scraps can match almost any pattern.

Even Arlene's husband has become involved in the surging interest in quiltmaking. Hank Vrooman is a master cabinetmaker and woodcarver, and his handmade quilting frames, cedar quilt storage chests and finely-wrought quilt display racks are sent to area craft stores and shows to rest side-by-side with Arlene's "Log Cabin" pot holders, "Fan" pillows, "Double Wedding Ring" table runners and one-of-a-kind wall-hangings.

By the summer of 1993, Arlene had made twenty full-size quilts on her own, and she had assisted her guild in the making of another ten quilts for charity and fund-raising—not a prolific number in itself, but impressive given the painstaking standards of craftsmanship involved in each one (they are all entirely hand-stitched) and all the other activities and projects competing for her time. She spends a great deal of time plotting a design. Even if she starts with a traditional pattern, she will add certain touches which make each quilt uniquely her own.

Her individuality and sense of artistic composition are perhaps best expressed in her pictorial quilts and wall-hangings. They are sometimes playful and whimsical; often they display a subtle and compelling poetic feel for symbolism. One wall-hanging, made as a tribute to American troops who served in Desert Storm, has an appliqued white dove with an olive branch against pieced strips in graduated pastel shades of desert sand and sky. It has the power, simplicity and compassion of great art.

One of her full-size quilts—Arlene's personal favorite, titled "Tribute to My Mother"—is a lyrical composition consisting of two appliqued pianos with musical notes swelling from the keyboards to form a heart. Arlene and her mother attended the same music school in Albany, twenty-five years apart. The border consists of small hands stretching towards the keyboards, representing the students taught by Arlene and her mother.

Even when using a traditional design, Arlene always adds embellishments to make it special, to put her own imprint or signature therein. One quilt, consisting of blocks of the ever-popular Depression-era "Fan" design, which she made entirely from period fabrics and reproductions, has a quilted rose in the corner of each block—a small touch to make the quilt stand out. As Arlene says, "Even if I take a pattern like the fan .... see, I'm gonna still add my thing to it." Creating a personal style within an established tradition is the mark of an artist at work in her chosen medium of expression. And Arlene described that special state of concentration an artist attains when the muse is near and the work proceeds with almost effortless ease:

> I usually quilt at night ... I just blot out everything around me, and that's what I mean by being serene. Just like you were sitting out in the woods where it's quiet and nothing but birds. It's just like you're into this, but you're not using the physical strength to make those blocks. My whole body is just being quiet. Any pain that I have, or anything like that—I'm not thinking about that. Everything is so calm, and I'm just sitting there quilting away. That's all I'm doing. [Arlene Vrooman, 1993]

"Basket Quilt" by Virginia Hull, hand-appliqued and tied in 1985. This 80" by 90" bed quilt was the second quilt Virginia made, a "penance" project undertaken to atone for inadvertantly ruining an heirloom quilt made by her grandmother. Virginia matched the materials, pattern and construction as closely to the original as she could. It went together so effortlessly, Virginia said, that it was as though her grandmother's spirit stood by and helped.

CHAPTER 8

Delaware County

The largest of the Catskill Mountains counties, Delaware is also the furthest west and, thus, the last to be settled. It wasn't until after the Revolution that a migration of homesteaders from New England and the lower Hudson Valley formed the first small communities, a scattering of hillside farms and tiny hamlets.

From this relatively late start, Delaware remains the most rural and agricultural of the five counties. The city of Binghamton lies just to the west, and I-88 skirts its northwestern border, but Delaware itself still consists primarily of neat and proud little villages spaced miles apart, with farms and forests surrounding and between.

Named for the river whose east and west branches have their headwaters in the county, Delaware is criss-crossed by streams and creeks, and its southern portion is dominated by two large reservoirs, the Pepacton and the Cannonsville.

Her economy was almost entirely derived from farm and forest products until the arrival of the Ulster & Delaware Railroad in the 1870s brought a sudden influx of tourists and boarders, giving temporary prosperity to a few villages along the way.

The tourist business remains important, as does farming, but neither industry appears destined, at this juncture, to ever again reach the levels of years past. The rocky hills of Delaware do not bode well for corporate agribusiness, and the quiet trails and trout streams cannot compete for the nation's recreational dollars with the hawker's hue and cry, the lights and glitz, of a theme or amusement park. Which is quite all right, one thinks, as one drives along Route 30 past the John Burroughs Memorial near the quiet stately hamlet of Roxbury.

Peg Barnes (b. 1930)

THE KING-SIZE (98" BY 98") QUILT WAS HAND-PIECED AND HAND-QUILTED BY PEG IN 1985. IT IS TITLED "SPRINGTIME BLOSSOMS," AND IS A VARIATION OF THE TRADITIONAL "HEARTS AND GIZZARDS" PATTERN.

*W*alk into any quiltmaker's home, and you will find yourself sur-rounded by art. There are the quilts, of course, in various stages of completion. But other forms of art or handcraft are usually in evidence as well, and most often they are further products of the hands and mind of the quiltmaker. "We have nests all over," Peg Barnes says, referring to the uncompleted projects inhabiting almost every corner of every room in the house in Arkville which she and her husband built themselves. Peg Barnes's oil paintings line the walls, looking down on her pieced and quilted vests, handbags and pillows, her pieced or appliqued tablecloths and place mats, her needlework and cross-stitch. And lying on the floor against one wall, almost over-looked in the happy clutter of works-in-progress, are her bagpipes.

Peg Barnes was born in 1930 in Bloomville, "a couple of moun-tains over" from her present home in Arkville. Her German and Scottish ancestors settled in the Catskills four generations ago. "Earlier, they were all farmers," Peg recalls, "but we've been in just about every kind of business you have, in later years"—a familiar Catskill Mountains pattern. And true to another frequent pattern, it was not Peg's mother, but her grandmother who provided Peg with her first glimpse of quiltmaking: "My grandmother, oh, she made so many quilts," Peg said, "and we were so used to seeing grandmother working with pieces. She did everything by hand." A prodigious feat considering that "Grandma had thirteen children," and not only quilt-ed for her own home but also made a quilt as a wedding present for each of her granddaughters.

Even with that early exposure to the art, Peg did not take up quilt-making herself until 1975. "I wanted something for the town for the bicentennial," she explained. "I didn't know a thing about it, other than the little bit I'd seen my grandmother do. So I made up twenty little packs—a piece of muslin, and a piece of batting, and a printed thing for the back—and I got nineteen different women in the town to make me a block." And the result? "I got everything. I had some that were embroidered. I got one that was needlepoint even. It's a unique quilt. But I have my quilt for the bicentennial."

The re-introduction to quiltmaking inspired by the patriotic fervor which swept the country in 1975, 1976—and the association of piece-work and patchwork quilting with traditional American folk art—more than any other single factor has led to the current and ongoing revival of quiltmaking in the Catskills. For many women who first worked on a quilt for the nation's 200th birthday, one quilt was not enough. Peg Barnes wanted to do more and learn more, so she joined the newly-formed Catskill Mountain Quilters Guild, which included some of the finest practitioners of the art: "The talent! This was Nina [Haynes] and Evadine [Garrison]! So I just asked questions. I learned so much from watching those women. That's really how I got into quilting."

Peg stayed with the guild, meeting with them every Monday morning to sit around the frame and help quilt on whatever group project they were working on, learning more all the time from the older and more experienced quilters on each side. She took classes and went to every workshop she could find. She attended meetings of the Wiltwyck guild in Kingston and then went on to join the Calico Geese in Sullivan County. She started to teach, giving workshops in schools and meeting with neighbors once a week to instruct them in piecing tops for tied quilts for donation to the new nursing home at the Margaretville hospital. Peg, a dedicated hand-quilter, almost blushed when she stated that they tie the quilts for that project, but she explained, "They have to have 84 of them!"

Peg Barnes still has her grandmother's quilt frame which she stores and brings out only when she is ready to baste the three layers of a quilt together. When the quilt is basted and marked, back goes the frame into storage. There are simply too many "nests" in her home to spare most of an entire room for a full-size frame. She then quilts in her favorite chair using a lap hoop for "a couple of hours." And then maybe she will do some cross-stitch or needlepoint or practice on her bagpipes. But those other arts and pastimes do not absorb her quite as much as does her quilted art. Of her quilts, and her quilts only, Peg Barnes reserved the comment, "I'm not wasting my time. I'm making heirlooms."

Phyllis Cameron (b. 1919)

THE 94" BY 86" BED QUILT, TITLED "INSPIRATION," WAS DESIGNED, HAND-PIECED, HAND-APPLIQUED AND HAND-QUILTED BY PHYLLIS OVER A THREE-YEAR PERIOD, COMPLETED IN 1994. PHYLLIS WROTE: "THIS QUILT IS MADE FROM SMALL SCRAPS OF LATE '30S OR EARLY '40S FABRICS FROM MY MOTHER'S SCRAP BASKET."`

$\mathscr{B}$orn on a family farm outside of South Kortright in 1919, Phyllis Cameron is a link in a great chain of family quiltmaking tradition which goes back at least three generations in Delaware County, and which she is passing on to her children and her grandson. Her mother was an expert quiltmaker who learned the art from Phyllis's great-grandmother. "I have clear memories of my mother working at the quilting frame in the parlor," Phyllis recalls. "We had a parlor then that we didn't use, only on special occasions. When I was small, I'd go in and play under the quilt."

When Phyllis was six or seven years old, her mother taught her piecing. A talented seamstress who made all of the family clothing, as well as all of the quilts for the family and the farmhands, Phyllis's mother used "no guideline or anything. She didn't make any marks; she just sewed. I don't know how she did it. I can't do it." Some of those quilts survive, and the quilting stitches sewn by Phyllis's mother in the 1920s and 1930s, without benefit of a guideline, are as perfectly straight as the stitches made by a master quilter today using a chalk-line or a straight edge.

And that is how Phyllis was taught to piece as a very young child in the mid-1920s–using no marks to guide her. And if it wasn't perfect, it just would not do. "We didn't have what we call a 'sewing line,'" Phyllis said. "[Today] we mark around a template with a pencil, and that's our sewing line. And then we cut it out and leave a quarter of an inch seam for the seam allowance. Well, we didn't do that then. We cut it out with the seam allowance, and I would have to attempt to sew across, sew two pieces together and sew it straight. Well, I'd start out real well, and then it'd go way down and my mother would make me rip it out and do it over again."

Phyllis continued to piece tops through her teen years until she married, but then she gave up quiltmaking until her retirement in 1983. Like many other women who learned to quilt at an early age in this century, Phyllis found no time to spare during the busy middle years. The demands of raising a family and working full-time at the college in Delhi (plus Phyllis and her husband had their own farm to run) precluded working hundreds of hours to produce a quilt. And quiltmaking was no longer a necessity; blankets and comforters had become inexpensive and readily available. As Phyllis said, "I guess I didn't organize my time like my mother did. She found time. She had to."

Then, in 1983, after Phyllis and her husband had retired, sold the farm and moved to Fraser, her best friend, Florence Tyler, took her to a Wiltwyck quilt show in Kingston, and the quiltmaking spirit was rekindled. She joined Florence Tyler's guild in Delhi, the Delaware County Historical Society Quilters, and between Florence's tutelage, working with other members of the guild, and her memories of her mother's strict instruction, Phyllis began to produce quilts that were a blend of tradition and inspiration, mixing piecing with applique, adding embroidery, crewel or cross-stitch to enhance the design.

Like her mother, who "always had boxes of pieces," Phyllis exercises the traditional quiltmaker's thrift. In the summer of 1993 Phyllis was working on a new top pieced from scraps left over from a top she had made when she was a teenager. Those fabric scraps had survived all those years, all the changes and transitions and the move to Fraser. "You know, it isn't as pretty as the cloth today," Phyllis stated, "and I sometimes wonder why I'm doing this." But she immediately answered her own question: "It's a challenge because they're all so much alike. There's no contrast, no dark and light to work with."

The challenge of it all—perhaps that is the best summation of Phyllis's approach to life. Quilting is hard on the hands, and Phyllis suffers from arthritis. But she has found a way to overcome that challenge as well, by quilting on a small floor frame in front of a comfortable chair at home rather than having to sit hunched over a large frame for hours at a time. And when even that becomes tiring there is always needlepoint, decoupage, crochet, latch-hook, plastic canvas, pressed flower pictures, beadwork, or one of the many other handcrafts which fill her home. Or maybe she will give her own hands a rest and spend a couple of hours teaching her grandson to piece, just as her mother had taught her to piece almost seventy years ago.

Eleanor Faulkner (b. 1904)

THE 85" BY 90" BED QUILT, "LAUREL LEAVES," WAS HAND-APPLIQUED AND HAND-QUILTED BY ELEANOR IN 1985. SHE REPRODUCED THE DESIGN FROM A SNAPSHOT A FRIEND HAD TAKEN OF A QUILT THEY HAD SEEN ON A TRIP TOGETHER THROUGH NEW ENGLAND. WHEN THE QUILT WAS COMPLETED, ELEANOR GAVE IT TO HER FRIEND.

"*I* don't have many of the quilts that I have made," Eleanor stated quite matter-of-factly, "for I take them to the quilt shows and generally they're sold before I bring it home." That statement serves as a tribute to the discerning taste and eye for value of visitors to Catskill Mountains quilt shows, for Eleanor Faulkner is one of the finest and most dedicated quiltmakers in the region. Her workmanship is exquisite, and her work habits are no less than amazing. "Eleanor gets up in the morning, starts quilting, and quilts all through the day and into the night," said one of her friends and co-workers in the Catskill Mountain Quilters Guild. That level of industry would be remarkable for a woman of twenty. For a woman who will soon be ninety, it is astounding.

Eleanor was born in 1904 in Dry Brook, "just over the line" in Ulster County. Her parents owned a small farm, and Eleanor remembers witnessing the coming of the modern age to the mountains: "We didn't have no electricity or any of those things. And I can remember when the first automobile came up the valley. Seems like a dream now."

When Eleanor married, she and her husband bought their own farm in New Kingston, Delaware County, where they raised cows and cauliflower. Eleanor recalls the difficult years struggling to maintain the farm and keep it economically viable: "The farms were small then. And each year you kept getting a little bit larger. You had to to keep going." They were caught in a vicious spiral. To keep pace with the changing economy, the farm had to expand year after year. And with the increase in size, more workers were needed. Finally, it became impossible to compete for wages and work conditions in a market-place where employment could then be found which was less rigorous and more rewarding than farmwork. As Eleanor said, "Got so that help was almost impossible to get on the farm. People wanted shorter hours and things. So we sold."

In 1954 Eleanor and her husband moved to nearby Margaretville, but the sudden release from the dawn to dusk daily tasks of farm life came as a shock. "I didn't have much of anything to do," Eleanor said. "When you're on the farm, your work is never done. You always have something left over for the next day. I was lost. I love to sew, so I took up alterations for the dry cleaner's down here." For many years

Eleanor continued to employ her sewing skills hemming skirts and pants for hire, occasionally working a bit of crochet or embroidery for her own pleasure.

Finally in 1980, at the age of seventy-six, Eleanor discovered quilt-making and her needlework blossomed into art. "We had quilts," she said, of her childhood back in the early days of this century. But her mother did not quilt, and Eleanor does not recall where those quilts came from or who made them. They were just there on the beds, useful objects of everyday living taken for granted. Eleanor's mother was a fine seamstress who made all of the clothes for her family, and she did teach Eleanor to sew, and to embroider and crochet, but not to make quilts.

For Eleanor, after a life spent with needle and thread always at hand, the transition from seamstress to quiltmaker was a smooth one. "You really do the same techniques in sewing and altering, and making things in quilting," she says. "The only difference is just that it's flat." She began by helping to quilt tops for her church in Margaretville, and then she joined the Catskill Mountain Quilters Guild in neighboring Arkville, where she can still be found every Monday morning.* Eleanor no longer drives, but her fellow quilters make sure that she gets there.

Since 1980 Eleanor Faulkner has made, or assisted in making, over fifty quilts. But don't look for them in her home. In the summer of 1993 Eleanor was just completing a "Maple Leaf" quilt: "This is my third one," she said. "I take it to quilt shows and I don't bring it home with me." She also quilts tops for other people to supplement her income and because "I love to sew by hand."

The four to six hundred dollars that a quilt often will sell for is a welcome addition to an income eroded by inflation and the low savings interest rates of the 1990s. But even so, "I have a few that I wouldn't part with," Eleanor says. Sometimes, however, the temptation is simply too great: "Last year, up in Roxbury, a party came to me and wanted to know how much I wanted for my quilt. And I said it wasn't for sale, and he said, 'Name your price.' And I said, 'It's still not for sale,' and he offered me a thousand dollars for it." I asked Eleanor if I could see this quilt that a "party" was eager to buy at virtually any price. "It's gone," she laughed. "I sold it."

On a gently sloping rise just outside the hillside village of Margaretville, Eleanor Faulkner rises each morning and goes to work. She sits at her small portable quilt frame and sews hundreds of tiny, perfectly spaced, perfectly straight stitches on the pattern she has traced on her own, or someone else's, quilt. Or she sits by the window hand-piecing from her scrap bag bits of brightly-colored calico into long strips to join together for her next quilt top. (How many pieces will she need for her design? "I don't know," she says. "There's oodles of 'em.") Having to make some concessions to age, Eleanor no longer walks the two miles into town and back, and she can no longer tend the vegetable and flower gardens she has always nurtured in the past. "I've had to give up a lot of things," she says, "and quilting's the only thing I haven't give up." [Eleanor Faulkner, 1993]

*Eleanor died in September, 1995, just before this book went to press.

Evadine Garrison (b. 1902)

PHOTOGRAPH 1985. COURTESY OF THE ERPF CATSKILL CULTURAL CENTER'S
FOLKLIFE PROGRAM.

It was fitting that the first induction for the new Hall of Fame in October of 1982 should include Evadine Garrison as one of the first to be honored. Evadine was one of those women who first inspired in Nancy Smith the idea that there ought to be a Hall of Fame for quilters. Not only was Evadine's work magnificent, and her support and coaching of less experienced or beginning quilters an inspiration, but Evadine Garrison was also one of the few Catskill Mountains quilt-makers of her generation who learned the art at an early age and then continued to practice it without interruption throughout her long life. During the middle decades of this century, when quiltmaking had all but vanished as a folk art of any importance, Evadine was making quilts, thereby helping to preserve the art, to keep it alive until the rebirth of interest in the 1970s.

In the early years of the twentieth century, many young girls were taught to piece quilt tops by their mother, grandmother, aunt or great-aunt. Sewing pieces of scrap fabric together is not physically taxing. Few learned to quilt before their teen years, however, because the effort involved in piercing three layers of fabric—which included a tough cotton batting and a coarse muslin backing—was usually thought too strenuous for a child's tender fingers. "To be a good quilter, you must prick your finger going down and coming up," Evadine was cautioned by her Aunt Jane, who introduced her to the art. And the exacting standards of quilting call for a proficiency in needlework that usually only comes with age and experience. Yet Evadine was quilting by the time she was nine years old.

Other interests came along, and Evadine left the Catskills for five years to study and work in Manhattan. But in 1928, when she married a dairy farmer from Arkville and returned to Delaware County to stay, she immediately resumed her quilting by joining the Women's Society of the Methodist Church in Arkville. She helped them finish quilts for the benefit of the church until the little group disbanded. She then continued on her own through all the intervening years until the next quiltmaking organization came to the area in 1975–Nancy Smith's Catskill Mountain Quilters Guild.

By that time, each of Evadine's children and grandchildren had already been given a quilt, and she was busy making "blocks practically every day" trying to keep up with the great-grandchildren.

Evadine's experience, knowledge and talent helped make the new guild a success. More and more women were drawn to the guild, and part of the attraction was Evadine's patient instruction and encouragement. Evadine has passed away, but her spirit still presides every Monday morning at the Erpf Catskill Cultural Center in Arkville, where the Catskill Mountain Quilters Guild now meets. Some of the women still in that guild, whom Evadine directly influenced and inspired, have since followed her into the Hall of Fame.

Evadine also joined Wiltwyck, making the long trip from Arkville to Kingston to participate in workshops, listen to guest speakers and share ideas with other quiltmakers. During her 60+ years of active quiltmaking, Evadine incorporated into her work piecing, trapunto and embroidery, and she made some wholecloth quilts. But it was applique which Evadine most enjoyed and for which she is best remembered today. The creation of a beautiful balanced design of great intricacy from nearly random scraps of fabric intrigued Evadine; "That, to me is such a rewarding thing," she said. She loved the challenge of working within a tradition, yet still finding a way to make each quilt new and unique, an expression of herself. "Although you may use a pattern, it's your own creative business that makes the thing tick." [Evadine Garrison, 1986]

Lois Gould (b. 1917)

THE 78" BY 95" BED QUILT, "CHURN DASH," WAS HAND-PIECED AND HAND-QUILTED BY LOIS IN 1995 FOR ONE OF HER GRANDCHILDREN WHO "REQUESTED A TRADITIONAL BLOCK FOR HIS QUILT."

ℒois Gould will not sell the quilts she makes because "You can't get what they're worth. It takes a long time to do the quilting if you do it by hand. I never have gotten into machine-quilting, and I don't intend to. If I can't quilt by hand, I won't quilt. To me, quilting is handmade." As with most quiltmakers, Lois has very definite ideas as to what a quilt should be and how it should be made. But she is also, again in common with most quiltmakers, very tolerant of how others approach the art. Lois prefers hand-piecing, but "just because I like it doesn't mean everybody has to do it. With quilting you please yourself. You don't please anybody else. Whatever you do. If you quilt a big stitch and you like that, fine."

Lois Gould did not become active in quiltmaking until 1981, two years after she retired from her post as clerk and treasurer for the Village of Delhi. But her roots in quiltmaking reach far back, all the way to her childhood during the Depression. Born on a small farm in Chenango County in 1917, Lois attended a "district school"–a one-room schoolhouse–where, in addition to the ABCs, the girls were taught "home arts." One of the projects Lois remembers making with the other girls in school was a "post card quilt," so-called because the top was pieced from remnants of cloth the size and shape of post cards. Those tops would then be padded, backed and tied by the class.

Her classroom skills were reinforced and refined at home under the guidance of her mother, a 4-H leader well-versed in many hand skills. Lois recalled her first experience learning to operate a treadle sewing machine. She and her sister would practice for hours on the machine with no thread in the spool. "We had to pump that machine, and we couldn't sew until we could do it at a constant rhythm," Lois said. "Mother would set and listen to us with that sewing machine. When we got so she would let us put the thread in, it was a big deal." Those were frugal days. Thread was too precious to waste on the trial and error of training. The self-sufficiency of the small farms in rural New York kept those families from feeling the full effects of the Depression but, as Lois added, "We never had so much of anything that we got tired of it."

Of course, frugality has always been an element in American quilt-making. And that tradition, when combined with the forced economies of the Depression, explains the resurgence of quiltmaking in the thirties. The refusal to discard anything that might possibly be made into something useful has endowed Lois Gould and her family with some rare heirlooms. One quilt top was made by Lois's mother around the turn of the century "from pieces of material she cut out of her mother's and grandmother's petticoats and skirts." Lois held on to that top until the early 1980s when she added the other two layers, quilted it and then presented it to her daughter.

But even more rare are the tops Lois saved that had been hand-pieced by her father when he was a young boy in the 1880s. Lois's grandmother was a professional seamstress who would take Lois's father with her as she made the rounds of the neighboring houses. She would then make him sit by her sewing machine in her workroom at home while she filled the orders she had taken. She taught him to piece the remnants she would cut and drop into the scrap basket "to keep him busy." Out of this child's play came some beautiful pieced quilt tops, one of which Lois and her mother later hand-quilted together in the 1930s. It is a work of collective family art spanning fifty years and three generations.

When Lois married and moved to Delhi in 1937, she continued to use her sewing skills to make clothes for her family, but she stopped making quilts. The middle years were busy ones for Lois. Besides, the surging wartime and post-war American economy brought affluence, even to the mountains. Quiltmaking had become associated with necessity and the long, cramped years of the Depression.

Forty-four years later, Lois returned to the art she first practiced as a little girl in that one-room schoolhouse in Chenango County. A friend convinced Lois to join the Delaware County Historical Society Quilters, and Lois's early training, combined with close observation of her new friends at work, soon had Lois producing the handmade quilts which would earn her a place of honor in the Hall of Fame.

Aside from using a lap hoop, Lois quilts today much as she quilted in the 1920s and 1930s. "I know I have funny ideas," she says, "but I like a traditional quilt done by hand." And her patterns are usually traditional as well: "I don't go for the fancy things they do today." Lois is fond of making wall-hangings, a recent addition to quilted art spawned by the growing recognition that the quilter's work deserves to hang alongside the more traditionally-accepted art of the painter or the draftsman. But, as with her full-size quilts which are gradually finding their way to the beds of every child and grandchild in her growing family, the wall-hangings are all carefully hand-pieced or appliqued, and they are all hand-quilted. "I don't think to be a good quilter that you have to be a perfectionist. But, of course, I think we're all inclined to be." [Lois Gould, 1993]

Marilyn Guy (b. 1932)

The 60" by 78" bed quilt, titled "Applique Sampler," was hand-appliqued and hand-quilted by Marilyn in 1994. It was her first attempt at applique, begun after she had learned the freezer paper method.

*M*arilyn was born in 1932 in Norwich, Chenango County, just west of the Delaware County Catskills. She spent her childhood and teen years there and in Garrison, a small town on the Hudson River 50 miles north of New York City, across the river from West Point. In 1956, shortly after she married, Marilyn and her husband moved to the village of Delhi, Delaware County. Her husband opened a pharmacy, and a few years later Marilyn opened a Hallmark card and gift shop which she operated until the winter of 1993. "I couldn't wait to get rid of it so I would have more time for quilting," she states.

There is a need within the human heart to proselytize. It can be one of the nobler enterprises of the spirit–a guiding hand reaching out to show others the way, to share the best that one has discovered. It is selfless, and often tireless. Marilyn Guy has become an apostle of quiltmaking. "I encourage anyone with the slightest interest," she says. "If I can do it, anyone can." Marilyn is an active member of the Delaware County Town and Country Quilters, hosts a small informal quiltmaking group in her home, gives private lessons and, she adds, "I also have a large library of quilting books and information that I invite area people to sign out and use on a regular basis."

The irony is that for many years Marilyn did not heed her mother's attempts to get her interested in the art. "My mother had always thought I would enjoy quilting," Marilyn explains. "I don't know how she knew. I had never liked sewing. I fought it so. Then my mother died in 1977." Perhaps because she is an only child, Marilyn was especially close to her mother and was devastated by her sudden death. "I was having a difficult time," Marilyn continues. "I decided to try it [quiltmaking], and it seemed to be my salvation. It took over my life really. I just did it all day, every day. It helped me through that grieving period."

Her first quilt was a "sampler" made, as she states, from "a botched skirt." The result may not have been a work of art, but Marilyn fell in love with the process. She joined Madeline Sanford's quiltmaking class at the Delaware County Historical Association after announcing to Madeline, "I want to make a 'Lone Star' quilt, and I hate to sew!" But Madeline was a patient instructor: "She tried to have structured classes, but we didn't conform," Marilyn recalls. Madeline would often get phone calls from Marilyn late at night, or first thing in the morning, and would coax her through one quiltmaking dilemma after another. "I give her credit for spurring me on," Marilyn says.

Gradually, as she immersed herself in the art of quiltmaking, her talents grew and her grief began to subside. "It makes me feel at peace," Marilyn says. "It is very relaxing. There is something about the fabric and the colors and designs that makes me forget any problems or stress." The complexity and variety of quiltmaking also appealed to her: "There are so many different steps in quilting that you never get bored," she adds. "You can be designing, choosing fabrics, making templates, cutting, piecing or quilting. When you are not in the mood for one part, you can always do one of the others. I'm usually working on several quilts in different stages. I like to have one that I'm piecing, one that I'm quilting, and one that I'm planning."

Over the past sixteen years Marilyn has made approximately 35 quilted works, including wall-hangings and baby quilts–a prolific number considering that much of her time is spent selflessly teaching and encouraging beginning quiltmakers, or lending her talents to the making of group quilts for her guild. And every stitch in every one of Marilyn's works is laboriously sewn by hand, although she states, "I'm trying to become machine-friendly."

Marilyn is a spontaneous artist who improvises as she works. She has tried plotting a design on graph paper and coloring it in, "But I don't stick to it," she says. "I usually don't have much of a plan. It just grows as I go along." But her improvisation is firmly rooted in tradition. Her chosen patterns are variations of traditional designs, such as the various "star" patterns, which she re-works as inspiration guides her. "I don't really care for contemporary," she states, adding that traditional quiltmaking appears to her to be a regional choice: "From what I have observed at quilt shows, I think we in the Catskills tend to be more traditional. You don't see the 'modern art'–contemporary–as often in this area."

Marilyn Guy is modest about her achievements. After stating that her applique work is not very good, she displayed a beautifully-designed and finely-crafted "Baltimore Album" quilt that she had nearly finished. Similarly, after being inducted into the Hall of Fame in 1986, just nine years after she first attempted to make a sampler quilt from "a botched skirt," Marilyn felt undeserving. "I never really felt comfortable or qualified for the honor. I'm not an expert seamstress. I just love the craft and encourage others to try it." It is the statement of an artist to whom one's own work never quite meets the expectations of the mind's eye (does it ever?), and whose passion for her art obscures the fact that her influence upon others has been profound.

Nina Haynes (b. 1896)

QUILTING ON A LAP HOOP. PHOTOGRAPH 1985, COURTESY OF THE ERPF CATSKILL CULTURAL CENTER'S FOLKLIFE PROGRAM.

*O*ne of the most prolific quiltmakers the Catskills has ever seen, and one of the most inspirational figures to the younger generation of quilt-makers in the northern county of Delaware, Nina Haynes was a natural choice for the first induction into the Hall of Fame in 1982. She was sponsored by no less than Bertha Mayes, co-founder of the new organization, who wrote of Nina's "perseverance" as being one of her special traits. "Perseverance" was a good choice of words because Nina, by that time, had made over 100 quilts, and all but a very few of them were hand-quilted. And that is just counting the quilts that Nina made completely on her own. As a member of the Catskill Mountain Quilters Guild, Wiltwyck and the Dry Brook Yesteryear Fair Organization, Nina had assisted in the making of another forty or fifty quilts.

Nina Haynes was eighty-six years old in 1982 when that information was presented to the board of directors of the Catskill Mountain Quilters Hall of Fame. What makes her productivity all the more remarkable is that, although Nina had by then lived a long and very busy life, she had not fully concentrated her talents on quiltmaking until after she retired.

In fact, Nina did not attempt her first quilt until just before she married in 1918. During an interview in 1985, Nina recalled that first experiment in quiltmaking sixty-seven years before: "I got this top off a woman for two dollars. Oh, it was gorgeous. I got wool batting to put in it and I tied it—I wore it out." It was a far cry from the hand-quilted works of art Nina was later to labor over for long hours at a stretch. That first quilt was obviously intended to prepare for the coming move with her future husband from the Millbrook farm on which she was born, in lower Dutchess County, to a farm of their own in Dry Brook, high atop the Catskill Mountains.

That Nina had not learned quiltmaking as a little girl at her mother's knee is understandable in light of the fact that Nina was but one of thirteen children on that little farm in Millbrook. But she did learn some sewing skills during her youth, and she continued to do "patching and family sewing" in her new home in Dry Brook. Then, in the 1940s, Nina's mother-in-law re-introduced her to quilting, which she was to continue to practice sporadically and "just for fun" from that time until she and her husband retired from farming. And then, with the house empty of children, and cows no longer grazing in the fields, Nina's hands, busy all her life, were idle. She began to occupy more and more of her time making quilts. It became a passion. It was a "godsend," she said in later life. And it was to become even more important in her life after her husband died. She would quilt until her "needles get hot," she said. And the friends she made through the quiltmaking guilds sustained her spirits as well. Nina's quilts were always traditional, and it was the actual quilting which she most enjoyed. About half of the over one hundred quilts she produced were appliqued, because she loved the delicate symmetric designs of the Pennsylvania Dutch quiltmakers. And applique always leaves the top with plenty of open areas in which to display the quilter's art.

Nina Haynes has passed away, leaving behind a rich legacy to the art of quilting. Half of her quilts were sold at craft and quilt shows during her lifetime. By now they are probably scattered throughout the country, those that have survived. The other half—over fifty in number—were given by Nina to family and friends, and many of those remain in the Catskills where Nina plied her art for almost seventy years. As Nina said in 1985, "You sit down to do it and you say, 'Well, I'll do a little more.' The more you do it, the more you like it. And then you look up at the clock and the time is gone."

Ethel Hinkley (b. 1895)

PHOTOGRAPH CIRCA 1985. COLLECTION OF THE CATSKILL MOUNTAIN QUILTERS HALL OF FAME.

*O*f all the inductees in the Catskill Mountain Quilters Hall of Fame, Ethel Hinkley is perhaps the one whose life—and whose life's work in quiltmaking—most closely resembled the quiltmakers of the early days of America. Ethel Hinkley began to make quilts because she had to. As she sat piecing a top for a quilt, she expected no further recognition nor reward for that work than the peace of mind which came from knowing that her family would be warm at night.

Quiltmaking was simply a part of her family's way of life when Ethel was growing up at the turn of the century. "My mother and my sister had always done it," she remarked in 1984. After her marriage at the age of nineteen, "the children commenced to come," as Ethel said, and "I had to have quilts for my beds." Ethel and her husband had moved to a farm in Meeker Hollow, Delaware County, where the winters were fierce and where sustaining a farm was a daily struggle. Economy was necessary, so quilts were pieced from the scraps left over from making clothes. "My mother always had pieced, so I started in," she said. "Some of them didn't look too good, but they were warm."

The children did, indeed, commence to come—thirteen in all. And they all needed quilts on their beds. Ethel remembered buying calico for five cents a yard to make the family's clothes. The remains and the scraps would wind up in the basket for future quilt tops. The clothes themselves would be recycled, sometimes ending up as pieces in the design on a quilt or, in the case of old coats, metamorphosing through Ethel's skill into children's winter play clothes. Thus did a large family survive on their own on a farm in the hills of Delaware County.

With time and the proficiency which comes with practice, Ethel Hinkley's quilts became more masterful and the quiltmaking less of a chore. "It was fun, although it was work," she said. As the years went by and the scrap basket overflowed, Ethel could afford to pay more attention to patterns and color schemes, until by 1976 she would be making quilts on the order of her bicentennial "Trip Around the World," pieced entirely with small uniform bits of red, white and blue fabrics.

Quiltmaking also provided Ethel with a social outlet and brief respite from the rigors of farm life and the demands of her large family—just as it always has done for American women. She belonged to an informal community group which would meet for quilting bees in members' homes. "We'd each take a block," Ethel remembered. "When we got enough, we'd put them all together and then quilt it. That wasn't a church group, but neighbors. Then we would give the quilt to some that needed it." Ethel Hinkley, with all of her own work to do, took the time to take part in that long-standing American quilt-making tradition of charity, generosity and social responsibility.

By the time she died in 1985, Ethel Hinkley had hand-made fifty-four full-size quilts and ten crib quilts. She sold only two of them, and regretted having done so. She preferred to give them to her children, grandchildren, great-grandchildren and, finally, great-great-grandchildren, as gifts of love to keep them warm and please their eyes. They returned that love and devotion, and they wrote a beautiful eulogy for "Grandma" Hinkley which reads, in part: "What we might see as a box of old left-over fabrics, she saw as a treasure just waiting to be put together in a beautiful pattern .... There was magic there, to feel hope and joy in those scraps."

Virginia Hull (b. 1937)

TITLED "RED, WHITE & GREEN," THIS 72" BY 72" BED QUILT WAS HAND-APPLIQUED AND HAND-QUILTED BY VIRGINIA, COMPLETED IN 1995. VIRGINIA WROTE: "THIS QUILT, WITHOUT THE BORDERS, WAS DESIGNED AS A CLASS SAMPLE FOR AN INTERMEDIATE APPLIQUE CLASS I TAUGHT."

*V*irginia Hull, one of the new breed of younger quilters to come to the art in more recent years, remembers her first instructor announcing, "I think we have a quilter here." That was in 1984. Virginia was inducted into the Hall of Fame just six years later, and by the summer of 1993 she had already completed 50 or 60 quilts and was one of the area's most sought-after instructors for all phases of quiltmaking. Virginia has no reservations about the status of quiltmaking in the 1990s: "It is my profession," she states. Virginia refers to herself and her fellow quiltmakers as "fiber artists."

Virginia's entire approach to quiltmaking is a blend of tradition and experimentation. Even her first impulse to begin making quilts was a variation on a traditional theme. "I always loved quilts," she says, "and I knew I'd never be able to afford one, so I decided to take a class and learn how to make one." Unlike the older generation of Catskill Mountains quiltmakers, Virginia did not have to make quilts in order to keep her family warm. But she was determined to have quilts on her family's beds for the sake of their beauty alone, and the only way for her to have them was to make them herself.

Virginia was born in Brooklyn in 1937. When she was fourteen, her father decided to move his practice out of the city and realize his life-long dream of becoming a country doctor. The family uprooted itself and relocated to the village of Grand Gorge, Delaware County. Having been born at the end of the Depression when quiltmaking was already in decline, and growing up in the comfortable middle-class security of a doctor's family, Virginia had little childhood exposure to quiltmaking. One of her grandmothers had belonged to a sewing circle in Brooklyn and made one quilt which has been passed down in the family. And Virginia remembers her family's housekeeper in Grand Gorge saving the scraps from the sewing machine to take home for use in quiltmaking. But Virginia had no direct early experience in, or exposure to, the art.

Virginia did learn from her mother how to knit and crochet, and before taking up quiltmaking in 1984 she had "tried every craft in the world," she said, including oil painting, ceramics, embroidery and crewel. Then Virginia took that first class in quiltmaking, taught in nearby Stamford by Victoria Faoro—who has since moved to Kentucky to become senior editor of *American Quilter's Society*

Magazine–"and that was it," Virginia said. "I was hooked." In quilt-making, Virginia discovered the form of self-expression she had searched for all of her life, and she immediately gave up all other crafts to concentrate on refining her quiltmaking skills.

Virginia bought every book on quiltmaking she could find. Then, after working on her own for a couple of years, she joined the Patchworkers in East Jewett, and then Wiltwyck in Kingston. Sharing ideas and skills with other women in the two guilds completed her education in quiltmaking, and Virginia began to pass on her new-found knowledge by teaching classes in guild workshops, in fabric and craft stores, and in her home. The money she earns from teaching buys the materials for her own quilt projects.

The inquiring mind and restless spirit that drove Virginia to try "every craft in the world" finds full expression in her quilted art. "I try every technique I can find," she says. Virginia is in agreement with "most of the professionals [who] say 'I break every rule there is.'" But rule-breaking is only for those who have already mastered an art. By her own industry and by studiously applying herself to learning every aspect of the quiltmaking process, Virginia has reached the point where she can stretch the boundaries of the art in her search for freer forms of expression. But the foundation must first be laid: "My private work is contemporary," Virginia says, "but my classes are usually traditional."

Virginia's traditionalism dictates that she hand-quilt, but she freely admits that quilting is not her favorite step in quiltmaking. "I just do that because you have to," she states. "While I'm doing it, I think about the next quilt I want to design." It is the planning and designing of a quilt which Virginia most loves, and she finds herself more and more drawn to quilted wall-hangings. Wall-hangings occupy a fraction of the time consumed in making a bed quilt, so one can move rapidly from one experiment in design to another. Wall-hangings are also an outlet for Virginia's latest interest–embellishing fabrics with weaving and tucking (or folding.) "With a bed quilt you're really stuck with being utilitarian," Virginia explains. "Even if you're not going to use it every night it still should be something that somebody might lie under and pull up over them. Whereas with a wall-quilt you can do anything you want with it. It's going to be up there on the wall, so you can do weaving and tucking and all that kind of stuff."

When an art ceases to develop, it dies. One of the reasons for the current worldwide quiltmaking revival is the breadth of technique and freedom of expression that is developing through the experimentation of quiltmakers such as Virginia Hull. The ancient art of quiltmaking is changing today more rapidly than at any time in its long history. And what is interesting about quiltmaking during this period of change is that the newer methods and designs are not supplanting the old. The traditional and contemporary coexist. "A lot of people are very traditional and they just want that calico quilt," Virginia says. Others, particularly the younger generation of quiltmakers, prefer bolder colors and original, often abstract, designs. Still others, like Virginia Hull, try to blend the traditional and the contemporary into something totally new and different, but with borrowings from the past. But whatever one attempts in the art of quiltmaking today, "there is a place for it," as Virginia says, "as long as it is well done."

Jeannette Hunt (b. 1905)

THE 81" BY 102" BED QUILT, "LAURIE'S QUILT," WAS HAND-PIECED AND HAND-QUILTED BY JEANNETTE IN 1995 AS A GIFT FOR HER GRANDDAUGHTER LAURIE, WHO CHOSE THE FABRIC AND THE PATTERN ("DAHLIA"). JEANNETTE WAS 90 YEARS OLD WHEN SHE MADE THIS QUILT.

*I*n relative obscurity, her mobility hindered by arthritis, Jeannette Hunt sits in her trailer on a hillside farm outside of Delhi and continues to fashion quilts in the 1990s in much the same way as she did in the 1920s. To watch Jeannette work is to witness living history, virtually undisturbed by time and by the recent innovations in quiltmaking. One of her latest works is a crib quilt made with a backing sewn from feed bags, a flannel blanket for the batting and, as for the top, Jeannette points out, "These are all blocks I had. This blue was a skirt my daughter had when she was going to high school. I used everything." The making of that crib quilt was not a self-conscious effort to recreate a Depression-era artifact using period materials. Jeannette put that quilt together in that manner, with those materials, simply because that is how she has always made quilts, from the days of her early childhood throughout almost the entire span of the twentieth century. "We made a lot of them like that," she says, referring to her generation of Catskill Mountains quiltmakers.

Born on a farm outside of Walton in 1905, Jeannette Hunt has spent her entire life in the rugged hills of Delaware County. It has been a life marked by continuity. Nearing ninety years of age, Jeannette proudly displays the vegetable garden she still tends, an annual summer activity she is determined, she says, to continue for "as long as I can dig up dirt." Her roots in quiltmaking run just as deeply.

On that first farm in Walton, Jeannette's mother made quilts for the family's beds and she taught Jeannette how to piece and tie, first doll quilts, and later full-size bed quilts. Jeannette took those skills with her when she married and moved with her husband to their own farm outside of Delhi in 1924. In common with most farm wives in the Catskills during that era, Jeannette made all of the clothes for her growing family, and the remnants and scraps were saved for quilt tops. The scraps were pieced into a traditional pattern–a "Nine-Patch," "Windmill," "Tumbling Blocks," or one of the star patterns–padded with wool, cotton or a worn flannel sheet or blanket, and then tied. They were intended to keep her family warm at night through the frugal use of leftover material, while still pleasing the eye.

With her move to the farmstead in Delhi, Jeannette joined the Spring Lake Missionary Society, a charitable organization of neighborhood women which began as a church-based society and then became non-denominational in order to include all local women regardless of religious affiliation. Each member of the Society would complete her own blocks at home and then bring them to the meetings, where the collected blocks would be joined together into a top, a backing and batting added, and the three layers would then be tied together. The Society donated the finished quilts to local fire victims in Delaware County, or they sent them to needy families as far away as Kentucky. They also made many crib quilts for the "Save the Children Federation" in New York City. "They'd send us the pieces and we'd send them back little quilts," Jeannette recalls. The Society continued until the fabric of American social life itself began to take on a whole new warp and weave in the 1940s. "In later years there were so many of the women out working," Jeannette explained. "For awhile we had meetings at night, but that was hard to go to and do all this work when they're doing other things. So we gave that up."

But Jeannette continued to make quilts on her own through all the coming years. Just as one season almost imperceptibly turns into the next season in the Catskill Mountains, gradual change did come into Jeannette's life. Her children grew older, married and had children of their own. When Jeannette and her husband retired, one of those grandchildren bought their farm and Jeannette moved out of the farmhouse and into the trailer on the hill behind it, almost within sight of the hilltop where Jeannette's husband's grandfather first settled and built a log cabin hand-hewn from virgin timber.

And some small changes did find their way into Jeannette's quilt-making. She had tied quilts all of her life, but in 1986 she began to hand-quilt, learning the art, she said, "by watching others." She still ties some of her crib quilts, but all of the large quilts are now hand-quilted, "mostly 'in the ditch'" [following the seams between the pieces in the top]. And after using a large floor frame for seventy years, Jeannette now quilts–"every day and night," she adds–on a lap hoop so she can work while sitting in a comfortable chair.

But the quilts themselves are pieced from fabric remnants into traditional patterns, just as they were in the 1920s. When they are finished they do not hang in quilt shows or appear for sale in craft stores, they are given away to family members just as they always have been. When asked how quiltmaking has changed over the last eighty years, Jeannette Hunt replied, "I don't know. Isn't quilting quilting?"

Emma Kelly (b. 1899)

WORKING WITH A LAP HOOP ON ONE OF HER EMBROIDERED QUILTS IN 1985. PHOTOGRAPH COURTESY OF THE ERPF CATSKILL CULTURAL CENTER'S FOLKLIFE PROGRAM.

*W*hen Emma Kelly was sponsored for induction into the Hall of Fame in 1984, her application listed her place of birth as Rose Mountain and her current address as Red Kill. Try finding either on a road map of New York and you will discover one of the small ways in which the twentieth century has changed our perspective of place. A topographical map will disclose both locations, but few but avid hikers or sportsmen possess such maps. Most of us are content with an atlas or state map listing major routes and larger towns.

If you grew up and lived your entire life (and ninety-plus years at that) entirely in the environs of the intersection of Greene, Ulster and Delaware counties, however, in the very heart of the Catskill Mountains, your world was small and your specific location was pinpointed. You did not live in Fleischmanns, but in Red Kill. You were born not in Pine Hill, but on Rose Mountain.

I would have been hard-pressed to find Rose Mountain without my topographical map, had my grandparents not built a summer cabin there before I was born. I remember riding up the dirt road on summer days in the late 1950s, with steep stone walls rising on each side of the narrow trail (so narrow two cars could not pass, in most places), thinking (as a "sophistocated" lowlander from the Durham Valley in Greene County) how wild and isolated Rose Mountain was. When Emma Kelly was born there at the turn of the century, it must have been an unspoiled paradise.

That mountain paradise would be reflected, in later life, in her quiltmaking. Emma was unique among the women in the preceding and ensuing pages, in that every single one of the 50+ quilts she created was neither pieced, nor appliqued, but all laboriously and beautifully embroidered in cross-stitch, and then quilted. Pastel embroidered flowers, leaves and ferns lie on a pure white muslin background. What do I remember of Rose Mountain? Leafy trees, wild flowers and ferns.

Emma was a link in an unbroken chain of folk tradition. She learned to piece tops and tie comforters from her mother and grandmother, while her mother-in-law taught her how to quilt. Emma, in turn, passed all of those skills on to her daughter, who, she once boasted, "can do anything."

Emma was a staunch Christian and, like many talented Catskill Mountains women of her generation, she joined the missionary society of her church, helping them make quilts during the 1920s and 1930s "to keep the church going. We'd just hang them out on the porch and people would stop and buy them just about as fast as we could make them," she recalled in a 1985 interview.

I regret not having had the opportunity to meet Emma, to talk about quiltmaking, the missionary society, Rose Mountain at the turn of the century, and to see in person, in living color, those pastel leaves, wildflowers and ferns come alive on a white muslin background.

Wanda Lanzi (b. 1918)

THE 85" BY 102" BED QUILT, "DOUBLE IRISH CHAIN AND HEARTS," WAS MACHINE-PIECED, HAND-APPLIQUED AND HAND-QUILTED BY WANDA IN 1995 AS A CHRISTMAS PRESENT FOR HER DAUGHTER AND SON-IN-LAW.

The New Kingston valley in northern Delaware County is off the beaten track. It is not far from Margaretville and the steady stream of tourist traffic on State Highway 28, but you have to look for this valley or you won't find it. Only one road goes into the valley, and what appear at first to be unpaved side roads branching off at infrequent intervals are actually long driveways which lead eventually to isolated farms, fallow and abandoned, or still struggling on. Steep hills rising up on either side of the road add to the feeling of isolation. It is quiet and serene. Ageless. One feels one could forget about time in a place such as this.

At the end of one long driveway is the farm where Wanda Lanzi came to work one day in 1935, when she was sixteen, and never left. The "No Parking" sign in front of the garage seems slightly ludicrous until Wanda explains that she lets hunters come and roam her fields in search of game. Sometimes she opens her house to them for room and board, and some of them have become good customers for her quilts.

In the fall of 1993, Wanda had several quilts in various stages of completion—some commissioned, and some as gifts for family members. "If I finish up what I got started, I gotta live to two hundred," she laughs. Her workroom appears understandably chaotic, but Wanda picks her way through it with ease and seems to know exactly where to find each fragment of fabric. When she says, "I've got enough material to open a store," it is almost an understatement.

Wanda was born in 1918 in the nearby village of Andes where her family had farmed for three or four generations. Many of those ancestral farmsteads are now under the still waters of the Pepacton Reservoir. Her father carried on the tradition, but the changing times made it necessary for him to schedule his farm chores around a full-time job at the Andes creamery. The rest of the family pitched in and they got by, but "it was kinda hard times," Wanda admits. "A quarter was a quarter in those days. When I worked out, I think the highest I got was $12 a week," she adds, "but I was makin' money." No mean feat in the heart of the Depression.

Wanda remembers quilts on the beds when she was a child, but "who made 'em, I don't know," she says. She remembers they were "mostly tied quilts—tied about four inches apart," and "they'd be warm." Anonymous and utilitarian, they were absolutely essential because Wanda recalls no blankets in the house at all—just the tied quilts.

When she was twelve, Wanda made her first quilt top, unaided by any instruction. "I wanted to sew," she recalls, "and so my foster mother said, 'Here's the material,' gave me a cardboard [to use as a template]—a postcard size, like—I guess that's 'brick' size, or whatever—and said, 'Now if you want to sew, you make yourself a quilt top.' So I did." A few years later, Wanda added a batting and a backing to her top, tied it together, and gave it to her sister as a wedding present. More than sixty years after that top was pieced, that quilt is still in use.

That first top must have satisfied for awhile Wanda's urge to sew because her next quilt was not made until 1938, when she was twenty years old. By then, she had moved to New Kingston on her own to work on the farm that she and her husband would eventually buy in 1945. An aunt in Walton coached Wanda through every step as she made two quilts—a "Dresden Plate" and a "Butterfly" applique. This time, both tops were quilted.

Wanda married soon after those two quilts were completed. The ensuing years followed the typical pattern of hard work around the farm and child-raising leaving little time left for quiltmaking. Sometimes, however, during the long winter months when there was less farmwork, Wanda would steal a few hours to work on a quilt.

But in the 1970s, Wanda began to make quilts in earnest and at such a pace that by 1993 she estimated she had made "200 or better." That number includes "baby quilts, crib quilts and doll quilts," Wanda says, and she freely admits that "a lot of them have been tied." Even so, it is a staggering figure.

One would expect to find quilts in abundance at Wanda's house, but that is not the case. "I haven't got much to show you," she says. "People call me and say, 'I want to come over and look at your quilts.' I say, 'What do you mean "look at my quilts?"' I say, 'I haven't got any.' I don't even have a quilt myself, really."

Those quilts that haven't been given away to her family have all been sold. Quiltmaking has virtually been a cottage industry for Wanda. Most of the quilts-in-progress in her workroom have been commissioned, including a king-size "Double Wedding Ring." "That's the second [king-size] one I made, and I don't want to make another one," she laughs.

As Wanda lists the different patterns she has used throughout the years, it is almost encyclopedic. The most popular patterns requested have been traditional standards like "Hearts & Gizzards," "Ohio Star," "Trip Around the World" ("Made quite a few of them"), "Clay's Choice," "Jacob's Ladder" ("That's another one I've made quite a few of"). Sometimes the work has been quilted, sometimes tied, depending upon the customer and the price, because "You can't charge the same for a tied quilt as you can a quilted quilt," Wanda explains. In line with the patterns she uses, Wanda's opinions on quiltmaking are traditional as well. She has tried machine-quilting, as an experiment, but she didn't like it; "If you want a machine-quilted quilt, might just as well buy one out of the store," she says. And when she quilts at home she uses a large old-fashioned floor frame. Her sole unorthodoxy—and an indication of her hardiness—is that she quilts *standing* up. "I always thought it was awkward sitting down," she says. Those long hours standing and *leaning* over a quilt frame—isn't that extremely hard on the back? "Well, I didn't feel it as much when I was younger," Wanda laughs.

Knee surgery two years ago has not stopped Wanda from regularly attending the weekly quilting bees of the Catskill Mountain Quilters in Arkville (of which she is a charter member), although she regrets that she hasn't been able to mow her lawn or do much gardening around the farm. She is also active in her church's Women's Circle, which makes tied quilts for nursing home patients. And she teaches novice quilters at an informal "Tuesday Night Group" in New Kingston, about which she is characteristically modest and matter-of-fact: "I don't know why anybody [who] can sew why they have to go to a class [to learn quiltmaking]," she says. "Like cooking—if you can read, you can do it."

In her 76th year and still tireless, Wanda Lanzi continues to be a source of inspiration, not only to her students, but to her peers as well—the experienced quilters of the Catskill Mountain Guild. She remains one of the cornerstones of that organization. Having made over 200 quilted works by herself, the growing demand for the guild's services leaves Wanda undaunted. One customer alone has 14 tops she wants the guild to quilt, "so we'll be busy for awhile," Wanda says with a smile.

Edna Moore (b. 1908)

PHOTOGRAPH 1985. COURTESY OF THE ERPF CATSKILL CULTURAL CENTER'S
FOLKLIFE PROGRAM.

"*Two* rooms in Edna's home in Hamden are proof of her sewing prowess," wrote Janis Benincasa in 1986. "Stacks of carefully papered floral print boxes line the walls. They contain needles and thread, fabric, pieced tops, and, in one case, hundreds of hand-sewn pieces of a 'Grandmother's Flower Garden' yet to be pieced together." That passage, extracted from *Catskill Mountain Quilters Hall of Fame*, published in 1986 by The Erpf Catskill Cultural Center, testifies to a long life dedicated to the full spectrum of sewing arts—from hand-sewn clothes to embroidery, tatting, quilting, even weaving. Those hundreds of tiny, meticulously hand-sewn hexagons of calico for a "Grandmother's Flower Garden" may never have found their way into a quilt, because by 1983 Edna Moore had given up quiltmaking for reasons of poor health. One only hopes that they were passed on to a still-active quiltmaker so that those expertly cut and sewn bits of fabric, saved as scraps and remnants for who-knows-how-many years, do not lie discarded or collecting dust in an attic somewhere.

Edna Moore's entire life was spent in the western Catskill Mountains. She was born in Shavertown in 1908 to a family well-versed in sewing skills. As a very young child, Edna was taught to sew by her grandmother, who was a professional seamstress in a shirt factory. The first results of that early tuition were clothes for her dolls, but as Edna was to state in 1986, sewing became "just natural for me." She became so adept with needle and thread that by the age of thirteen she was not only quilting, she had also already begun to receive commissioned work as a professional seamstress.

When Edna married in 1930, she and her husband moved from Delaware County to the small village of Youngsville in Sullivan County. Although Edna had learned the basics of quiltmaking years before, it was by joining the Ladies Aid Society of the Youngsville Presbyterian Church that her skills were to blossom in a communal atmosphere of fellowship, mutual support—and very hard work. The Ladies Aid Society was extremely prolific. "Each member would piece (or applique) tops," Florence Tyler wrote in 1983, when she nominated Edna for the Hall of Fame. "Then they quilted them as a group, doing 20-30 per year, averaging one quilt about every two weeks." That experience with the Ladies Aid not only helped Edna refine her quilting skills, it also instilled a quality which was to stay with Edna for the rest of her life–helping others. When Edna eventually moved back to Delaware County, to the village of Hamden, she began to make quilts for the Delaware County Infirmary in Delhi, and then joined the newly-formed Delaware County Historical Association Quilters, sharing her knowledge along the way with anyone willing to learn the art. As Florence Tyler wrote in 1983, "Just mention quilting to her and you have help; the 'ball' starts rolling."

Edna Moore's quiltmaking and her instruction were, self-admittedly, "quite exacting." She preferred accuracy over inspiration, working always within tradition. For Edna it was perfectly-mitered corners, even cutting and piecing, straight binding and a close, even quilting stitch that bespoke true refinement of the quilter's art. As she stated in 1986, "That's just my way of doing things ... It's got to be done good or I wouldn't do it."

Edna Moore never sold her quilts. They were given away as gifts or donated to various charitable causes. Much of her work was in contribution to group-made quilts which were then raffled off to benefit the Youngsville Presbyterian Church or the Delaware County Historical Association, or given to adorn a bed and comfort the spirits of a patient at the Delhi infirmary. Her art lies scattered throughout the Catskills. Much of her quilted work which has survived would be as anonymous as an individual artisan's contribution to a medieval cathedral. Her legacy best survives in the lives and works of the younger quiltmakers she influenced and inspired, and to whom she selflessly gave of her time. And, finally, there is that box filled with small bits of calico, cut and sewn into tiny hexagons, waiting for still-able hands to complete the work Edna Moore began.

Astrid Ormiston (b. 1908)

PHOTOGRAPH TAKEN THE DAY OF HER INDUCTION IN 1988. COLLECTION OF
THE CATSKILL MOUNTAIN QUILTERS HALL OF FAME.

*I*t is a tribute to the demographic diversity of the Catskills that the only sisters thus far inducted into the Catskill Mountain Quilters Hall of Fame were born, not in Kingston or Catskill, Stamford or Liberty, or in any of the other riverside or mountaintop villages in the region—but in Sweden. Astrid Ormiston was born in 1908, two years before her sister Viola Scranton, and she entered the Hall of Fame in 1988, two years after Viola was inducted. As young children, the sisters made the long ocean voyage together when their parents emigrated to America in 1915. They played together in the streets of New York City, gradually learning the language and mores of their new country. Then they again moved together in 1920, this time to a farm in the rocky hills of Delaware County—a land as strange and foreign from their adopted new world of New York City as New York City was from Sweden. They both learned quiltmaking in 1932, though they were miles apart by then, and in 1993, when Astrid was grievously ill, it was Viola who sat by her bedside taking notes for this biography from the older sister she had nominated successfully for the Hall of Fame in 1988.

Life on the Blenheim Hill farm in Delaware County where Astrid spent her teen years left little time for the finer arts of sewing. The entire family was kept busy with the continuous round of daily chores which kept the farm functioning. With seven children to tend to, and her husband often forced to work off the farm to make ends meet, Astrid's mother had no time or energy left by the end of the day. Because women with large families—and especially farm wives—were inundated with work, many children of Astrid's generation learned sewing from their grandmothers. But Astrid's grandparents were in Sweden, six thousand miles away. What early sewing skills she did acquire, Astrid learned with her sister Viola in the country schools and 4-H clubs they attended; the rest was self-taught, built on that foundation.

Astrid had no quiltmaking experience when, in 1932, she saw a pattern for a floral applique quilt top in *Good Housekeeping* magazine. She sent away for the pattern and when it arrived, she said, she simply "followed the directions." Out of that moment, when the pattern in the magazine caught her eye, grew a lifelong means of artistic expression which occupied Astrid's spare time for almost the next sixty years, ending only with her ill health in the 1990s. She produced about thirty quilts, most of them appliqued, and all of them hand-quilted. Like her sister Viola, Astrid never sold any of her quilts. She made them for her children and grandchildren, or stored them away as future presents for occasions yet to arise. She was a traditionalist in an art of long-standing traditions.

Astrid left the family farm on Blenheim Hill when she married, moving with her husband to the town of Vestal, near Binghamton. She used her education from Albany Business College to help support her family by working in banks or as town clerk, all the while continuing to make quilts and learning to crochet, embroider and knit along the way. After fifteen years in Vestal, Astrid and her family returned to Delaware County, to the village of Stamford, where she stayed for the rest of her life.

In addition to being a working mother, Astrid Ormiston was an active member of her community, but she never joined a quilting group or guild. No doubt she shared ideas with other quiltmakers, particularly her sister Viola, but Astrid was a solitary quilter, working quietly on her own, creating quilted works of art to "give as presents to her family." Competition for selection to the Hall of Fame had become more intense by 1988. It was no longer considered enough just to be an expert quilter. More and more emphasis was being placed on sharing skills and knowledge through instruction or community participation. But in an election year that saw only two women chosen for induction, Astrid Ormiston–unaffiliated with any quilting organization–was one of them. Her work was simply too good to pass over. She had no pretensions nor expectations for her quiltmaking, other than the simple yet eloquent desire, as she told Viola Scranton in the summer of 1993, "to make something beautiful."

Elsa Sanford (b. 1914)

AT WORK ON A "LOG CABIN" IN 1985. PHOTOGRAPH COURTESY OF THE ERPF CATSKILL CULTURAL CENTER'S FOLKLIFE PROGRAM.

*I*n the fall of 1993 at her daughter's floral shop in Fleischmanns, Elsa Sanford had her quilts displayed for sale. Suspended from the ceiling, they looked quite at home among the roses and chrysanthemums, the entire scene a fitting blend of art and nature. Elsa presided cheerfully over the sale, greeting customers as they strolled in, glad to talk about quiltmaking. She had recently sold her house and she simply did not have room anymore for so many quilts.

Elsa Sanford had made and sold many quilts over the past 40 years—nearly 300 in all, by her reckoning—and she could watch the last few go without sentiment. For Elsa, it is the process of making quilts that is important, more so than the finished works themselves. "It seems as though I can't leave fabric alone, you know? I just like to get my hands on it," she says.

Her current project is the completion of many unfinished quilts she had started and then abandoned over the years. "When they came to clean out my house down here two months ago, here's box after box after box of unfinished products, or quilt pieces cut for some certain thing." Elsa has already completed a "Double Wedding Ring" wall-hanging from one of those boxes, and she is working on two quilt tops, a "Necktie" and a "Trip Around the World." Although now in her eightieth year, one gets the impression Elsa could still replace those quilts in the floral shop almost as fast as they sell.

Elsa Sanford was born on a farm in New Kingston, Delaware County, in 1914. By 1993, she had lived in those environs continuously for 79 years, and she had witnessed many changes. As a child, Elsa remembers, "There was 40 or 50 farms up in New Kingston at that time. Now there's two." Farming, she adds ruefully, is "kind of an uphill business."

But precisely because it was such a struggle to maintain a small family farm in Delaware County during the early days of this century, quiltmaking thrived. It was still less expensive to make a quilt than to purchase blankets. It was also a traditional method by which women were able to express sympathy and support in a tangible and practical fashion to neighbors in distress. Elsa still has an heirloom quilt in her collection which was made in 1906 for her grandparents when their home was destroyed by fire. It is an unusual work because instead of cotton or wool for a batting, it is stuffed with paper. "Neighbors were friendlier then," Elsa comments. "Now everybody's too busy watching TV."

Elsa had one grandmother and one aunt who made quilts, but perhaps because her own mother was not a quiltmaker, Elsa did not learn the art until later in life. The closest Elsa's mother came to quiltmaking was the tying of comforters. There was no piecing or pattern involved at all; Elsa's mother would simply buy two large pieces of material, sandwich cotton in between, and tie them together. It was about as rudimentary as "quiltmaking" can be, but at least it provided the young Elsa, working side-by-side with her mother, with the basic idea of quilt construction. Elsa remembers the difficulties of working with the old cotton battings: "In those days cotton was not in a roll, like it is today. It came in a big bag, and you had to take it out by little tufts, you know, and lay it on. And then, of course, the first time it was washed, there goes all the cotton in heaps! So we had to tie it quite close—I don't know, a couple of inches, or maybe less—to keep the cotton in place." It was not nearly as time-consuming as quilting, but such close tying would take a couple of days because, with all the other work to do on the farm, "we wouldn't get at it until after dinner," Elsa recalls.

It was just another chore, really; there was no art involved. Consequently, 40 years passed before Elsa found herself seated once again with a quilt frame in front of her. Her hands were busy in the interim fashioning clothes for herself and her children. She dabbled in knitting, embroidery and crochet, but only as occasional pastimes.

Then one day in the late 1950s, as Elsa relates, "My friend called me up and said, 'Elsa, come on over. I got a quilt on.'" Her friend taught her how to piece a quilt top and how to quilt it together, and Elsa was soon hooked. "I just got to liking it so much that I would go home, cut out a few pieces and start in on quilts," she says.

Elsa learned quickly. Her friend became sick and entrusted Elsa to finish a commissioned "Log Cabin" quilt for her. "And then," Elsa says, "I had a sale of a 'House' quilt—each block was a house—and I made that for a man. He gave me a hundred dollars for it. 'Course, that was a big price in those days." Now Elsa was *really* hooked. What had started as a pleasant pastime soon became a one-woman cottage industry.

The commissions started to stream in and quiltmaking became Elsa's full-time activity. "I'd usually quilt from eight o'clock in the morning–now, that was when I was feeling good–and stop and get a little lunch and supper, and I'd quilt lots of times until eleven at night," she says. "I could quilt a quilt in three weeks."

Elsa made many, many quilts from scratch. She also sometimes teamed up with her sister, Bertha Mayes, who later became a co-founder of the Catskill Mountain Quilters Hall of Fame. Elsa would piece the top together, and then Bertha would do the quilting. Elsa also solicited quilt tops from other people by placing an ad in the local newspaper. If a top was of good quality, Elsa would buy it, add a backing and a batting, quilt it together and add the finished quilt to her inventory.

Elsa worked steadily, whether or not she had an order to fill. She would take her quilts to area fairs where they would usually find a buyer or stimulate more commissions. Elsa remembers one venue where she had particularly good success: "We had what we called the 'Whoop-de-doo' in New Kingston. Jeepers, we had as many as 3000 people there on the day of the 'Whoop-de-doo.'" Over the years, many a Whoop-de-doo-goer would leave at the end of the day with an Elsa Sanford quilt tucked under his or her arm.

Elsa's fame spread. In 1965 she was invited to give a one-woman show at the Erpf Catskill Cultural Center in Arkville where she had 30 of her quilts on display. When Nancy Smith started the Catskill Mountain Quilters Guild, Elsa was one of the first to be invited to join. Then, in the 1980s, Elsa embarked on a rigorous teaching schedule, giving an 8-10 lesson course in quiltmaking in five area towns–Grand Gorge, Andes, Roxbury, Arkville and Hamden. Quiltmaking had reached a peak in popularity. One little town had so many applicants for Elsa's course that she had to divide the class into morning and afternoon sessions.

All the while, Elsa continued to make quilts. Her patterns were traditional; the "Log Cabin" design became her specialty. ("That's the one I made the most of," she says. "It's fun to put the colors together.") Other favorites were "Windmill," "Rocky Road to Kansas" and "Maple Leaf." Elsa prefers piecing to applique; "I love to cut pieces, and I like to fit them together and have them come out in a pattern," she says. Another favorite is "Grandmother's Flower Garden," a very precise and labor-intensive design involving hundreds of tiny cloth hexagons stitched together, which Elsa, at the age of 79, has just begun another version of, dismissing the difficulty with the comment, "There's a little trick to it, then it goes together just like butter on bread."

After 40 years of quiltmaking, and 300 quilts, Elsa was asked if she did it for pleasure or for money. "It's both," she responded. "I did it because I like to do it, and if you can sell it, why not get the money?" Elsa enjoys knowing that her quilts are in homes all across the country. One crib quilt even went to Africa. Senator Jacob Javits and former New York Governor Malcolm Wilson were each presented with a quilt. And each member of her family has been given one, including all the grandchildren and great-grandchildren.

Elsa remembered a few times when she was so pleased with how one of her quilts turned out that she hesitated to sell or give it away. But then she shrugged her shoulders and said, "Well, sugar! I can make myself another one." And off it went.

It is the process of quiltmaking that matters to Elsa—getting her hands on the different fabrics and seeing the patterns take shape. She has adapted to her new life in an adult home, dispensing with her large frame and learning to use a smaller snap-frame. Next, "I'm gonna learn to do it on a hoop," she announces. Elsa Sanford is an artist who will continue to create as long as she possibly can, fashioning geometric designs of beauty out of piles of cut up fabric, and then quilting through that design because, as she says, "Quilting gives it life."

[Elsa Sanford died in 1995]

Madeline Sanford (b. 1903)

Photograph 1985. Courtesy of the Erpf Catskill Cultural Center's Folklife Program.

Two Stones For Every Dirt, a recent book on the history of Delaware County, offers poetic testimony to the rigors of trying to live off the land in the northwestern Catskill Mountains. That same rock-strewn landscape, however, has proven to be very fertile ground for quilt-making, nurturing from as far back, at least, as the mid-1800s a strong and county-wide tradition stretching in an unbroken line, unaffected for the most part by national trends and fads.

Madeline Sanford was born into that tradition in 1903, and her life and work were to become a legacy which would leave Delaware County and its quiltmaking tradition richer and more vital than ever. Her apprenticeship in quiltmaking may be traced back to Arkville in 1907, when Madeline was only four years old. Her mother—who was to live for only one more year—showed Madeline how to piece and tie a miniature quilt for her "string doll." The next year, after her mother died, Madeline went to live with an aunt who continued to encourage Madeline's quiltmaking in order, as Madeline was to say, "to keep me out of mischief." By the age of ten, Madeline was piecing and tying bed quilts, sometimes with the help of her younger brother.

Those early skills were to come back into use when Madeline married in 1922 and suddenly found herself in the position of having to furnish her own home. She pieced some tops during the long winter months and, in the spring, when Madeline and her husband moved into a new house with "great big, light rooms upstairs," as she would state during an interview in 1986, "I could put my frames up and just leave them all summer." The luxury of having a separate room to set up her quilt frames was all Madeline needed to embark on a sixty-year career in quiltmaking. "I quilted I don't know how many quilts that [first] summer," she said.

In the years to come, Madeline's quilt frames were always in use. By the end of her life, Madeline had made over fifty quilts, most of them hand-quilted. She had also assisted in quilting many others through her participation in guilds and church groups. As Jeanne Shaw wrote when she nominated Madeline Sanford for the first Hall of Fame induction in 1982, Madeline "belonged to Ladies Aid groups and church organizations which always had one or more quilts in the making."

Those societies and church organizations, together with forty years' service in the 4-H, kept Madeline continuously active in quilt-making during the middle years of the twentieth century, when quilt-making was a dying art in most of the rest of the country. Madeline was one of the very few experts in quiltmaking available when the art again became popular in the early 1970s. In 1976 she founded the Delaware County Historical Association Quilters, still one of the largest and most active quilting guilds in the northwestern Catskills (though relocated and renamed the Delaware County Town and Country Quilters). Madeline Sanford's influence and example are still revered in that organization; it is as though she still presides today, years after her death.

Acknowledged as one of Delaware County's experts in the art, Madeline was called upon to judge quilts at the Walton Fair, and she started her own classes in quiltmaking, both in Delhi during the warmer months, and in Florida in the winter. She helped found the Catskill Mountain Quilters Hall of Fame in 1982 and was enthusiastically inducted the first year.

"Quilting her way through life," is how Jeanne Shaw described Madeline Sanford back in 1982. From her mother's first instruction at the age of four, through her quilting out of necessity as a young woman in the 1920s and 1930s, her membership in ladies aid societies and 4-H during the middle years of the century and, finally, the founding of her own quilting guild in the 1970s, the story of Madeline Sanford's quiltmaking career encapsulates the history of quilting in the Catskills in the twentieth century.

Florence Tyler (b. 1920)

THE 84" BY 96" BED QUILT, TITLED "MY BALTIMORE ALBUM," WAS HAND-APPLIQUED AND HAND-QUILTED BY FLORENCE IN 1991. FLORENCE WROTE OF THIS PRIZE-WINNING QUILT: "WENT TO A CLASS FOR PAPER APPLIQUE. EXPECTED TO MAKE A PILLOW. CHANGED MY MIND."

"*I* was fixing a dress last night for a girl the same age as my grand-daughter," Florence Tyler said in the summer of 1993. "It's two inches too long on the shoulders." Then she added, with incredulity, "And her mother couldn't do it!" To Florence, it was like discovering that somebody didn't know how to boil water.

There are always differences between generations, however. Were it not for the quiltmaking revival in the 1970s, sewing might rapidly have become one of the moribund home arts. Instead, the reawakened interest in quiltmaking has occasioned a corresponding boom in homemade clothing. Pieced, appliqued and quilted vests, shirts, dresses and jackets—employing not only cotton remnants, but articles like silk ties and chenille bedspreads—have become a staple at quilt shows and in craft shops and galleries. In the past, women in the Catskills made their quilt tops from leftover dressmaking fabrics. Now they make their clothing from leftover quiltmaking fabrics. The inspiration remains the same—the serendipity of materials at hand.

By 1993, Florence Tyler had made 75 quilts. Her quiltmaking had earned her widespread recognition, prize ribbons at shows and induction into the Catskill Mountain Quilters Hall of Fame. She had sold much of her work, earning up to $1000 for a quilt. But she was perhaps best known for her quilted vests, of which she had made nearly 100, many of them "using a 12 inch Celestial Star block on the back," she wrote, "and one-half of the 8 Point Star on front, then one inch strip-piecing to complete the vest. The vests have gone from Maine to California, N.Y. to Florida. The Star block is pieced by hand, the strips added by machine. Then hand quilt the blocks."

Florence speaks and writes with a terseness and clarity that bespeaks her 23 years teaching home arts as a 4-H leader. She gets her point across directly and succinctly, and has become a sought-after quiltmaking instructor, teaching workshops within the Calico Geese Quilters Guild in Liberty and at the Cornell Extension in Hamden. One of her classes on making quilted vests grew into an informal guild—G.A.L.S of Delhi (the Gabbing And Laughing Society).

Florence was born in Goshen, Orange County, in 1920. Her family was relatively prosperous until the Depression hit. Her father, who was an insurance and real estate broker, "lost everything when the banks closed," Florence relates. But the family picked themselves up and carried on; her father became a traveling salesman, and her mother's work as a county leader in the Home Extension (the "Home Bureau" at that time), specializing in furniture upholstery, was little affected by the crash. "We had plenty," Florence recalls, "but it was hard work."

One of the ways the family made ends meet was by Florence's mother making dresses and coats for herself and her daughters. Florence remembers wearing "a lot of hand-me-downs, but we didn't feel bad about it. I mean, she'd remake them, and we'd have clothes." By the time she was in the eighth grade, Florence had learned to sew and make clothing herself, and she became a leader in 4-H the next year. Skills learned in school were applied at home, with Florence and her siblings expected to help their working parents keep the household functioning. They helped with the meals and the sewing, Florence recalls, and she finds herself impatient with today's generation: "I think it's ridiculous when kids have nothing to do," she says.

With this background, it is a little surprising that Florence did not grow up in a quiltmaking environment, but neither her mother nor her grandmothers made quilts. Her great-grandmothers had quilted, and a couple of their works remained in the family, but the art skipped 100 years and two generations until Florence began to make quilts in the early 1970s. Her mother's sole attempt was a tied quilt that she made in the early 1940s for Florence and her husband shortly after they married. It was filled with cotton batting left over from stuffing furniture, and the top was made from remnants of furniture upholstery which she "extended with sateen," Florence recalls. It may not have been a work of art, but it "kept us warm for a number of winters," she adds.

By then, Florence had graduated from Delhi Tech, Delaware County, and had settled permanently with her husband on the Delhi farm on which he had been born. Looking back, in 1993, Florence remarked about the changes she had seen in the northwestern Catskills: "There's only three farms where there used to be thirty farms." The Tyler farm is one of those that is no longer functioning, Florence and her husband having sold their dairy herd and retired in 1978. Afterwards, Florence's husband bought a couple of mules and a couple of oxen to have around because, she says, "He got lonesome for animals after he sold the cows."

As a young farmwife in the 1940s, Florence almost became a quilt-maker, out of necessity. "We needed blankets," she recalls. "We had blankets that needed a cover, so I did piece a few little tops, and then covered the blanket with it. Tied them. Nothing great. It was just another cover for the bed." It did, however, partially satisfy Florence's need to be creative during days otherwise filled with repetitive chores. It "gave me something to do, too," she adds. "That was before I went to the barn to milk. After I went to the barn to milk milk, forget it. There's no other time."

Florence continued to make clothes, and she would occasionally occupy her spare time with macrame, crochet or knitting. Her seamstress skills were constantly in demand in the Delhi area, and she remained very active in 4-H. It was through her 4-H den that Florence finally turned her talents to quiltmaking. "In 1970, in our home den group, one person wanted to know how to do a 'Cathedral Window,'" Florence explains. "I said, 'I know how'–big mouth, you know? I couldn't find the magazine I'd seen it in, but I had a sample that I had made at the time thinking, 'Yeah, that'd be fun to do.'" From that sample, Florence was able to recreate the steps involved in its construction and teach her den how to replicate it.

It took Florence until 1975 to finish that one "Cathedral Windows," but by the time she was done, she knew the basics of piecing quilt tops and was ready to do more. "At that time, I had no quilting books or magazines for ideas, and no quilting group," Florence says, so her next top was an imitation of a "Broken Dishes" that her great-grandmother had pieced a century earlier.

Florence would probably have continued making a few quilts on her own, solely as an occasional hobby, were it not for Madeline Sanford organizing the Delaware County Historical Association Quilters in the mid-1970s. Florence didn't join the guild until 1979, after she and her husband had retired from farming, but the results were immediate: "I learned a great deal," she recalls. With her considerable needlework talents and experience, all it took was a little coaching in quiltmaking methods, and Florence was soon turning out prize-winning quilted art.

She also found that her new art was marketable. "Besides enjoying sewing, it was something I could do for added income," she states.

"More satisfaction, less stress than dressmaking. If they want to buy it, alright. If they don't, that's alright too." Many of her quilts, and most of her quilted vests, have been sold, but she does not let financial considerations influence her sense of ethics. Once, a potential customer offered her $1000 for a quilt she had been commissioned to make for only $600; she turned down the higher bid. Those items Florence doesn't sell, she gives away as gifts.

Over the past twenty-three years Florence has experimented with different styles and methods such as "Stained Glass" quilts, "Celtic piecing," "Japanese piecing" and "English piecing." She produces fine applique work, but she prefers piecing because she can carry it and work on it wherever she goes. Regardless of the style or technique used for the top, the finished work is always hand-quilted, usually by the "quilt-as-you-go" method (again because she likes to take her work wherever she goes).

At 73 years of age, Florence shows no signs of slowing down. She is active in three quilting guilds, and is an active member of the Hall of Fame. She is a judge of quilts, and a stern judge at that; when asked if it was difficult to give low marks to another quiltmaker's work, knowing well the hundreds and hundreds of hours that go into a hand-stitched quilt, Florence replied, "So what? It has to be good work."

Her own work shows no sign of decline. She finished a "Baltimore Album" quilt just in time to submit it for judging at the Calico Geese quilt show in the summer of 1993 and walked away with a blue ribbon. She stays busy, and filling orders for quilted vests does not force her to neglect her quiltmaking. "I'm doing quilts all the time, but vests all the time too," Florence states. "I've got a half dozen things going all the time." Unlike retirees who waste away in boredom and idleness, Florence remarks, "There's not enough hours in a day!"

Marie Kremer

MARIE KREMER, 1995. THE TWIN-SIZE BED QUILT, "TWINKLING STARS," WAS HAND-PIECED AND HAND-QUILTED BY MARIE IN 1994 AS A GIFT FOR HER GRANDDAUGHTER. THE TOP WAS PIECED FROM SCRAPS, AND THE DESIGN CONSISTS OF "OHIO STAR" WITH A "LOG CABIN" CENTER.

CHAPTER 9

Epilogue

18 September 1994. Delaware County Fairgrounds, Delhi. The paddocks and parade grounds are empty. The first chill of autumn is in the air, and the hills surrounding the level flats of the fairgrounds are tinged with what will soon be a blaze of bright colors, harbinger of the onset of an early mountaintop winter. At the far corner of the grounds, one parking lot has about forty cars. Two small barns are filled with people in this otherwise-deserted scene, and the rafters inside are draped with the bright blaze of patchwork quilts.

It is a well-chosen setting for a quilt show. Against the rough dark wood, the variegated quilts display extremely well. One barn houses the biennial quilt show of Delhi's Delaware County Town and Country Quilters Guild—a rich cornucopia of the fruits of current talent, side-by-side with antique collections giving homage to the past.

The second barn is devoted to the Catskill Mountain Quilters Hall of Fame 1994 induction ceremony. It is an intimate gathering, like an extended family reunion. A sampling of quilts made by this year's five honorees adorn the walls, together with quilt blocks made for the Hall of Fame by the previous 41 inductees. Again, past and present are given equal time in this celebration of the changing—yet traditional—art of Catskill Mountains quiltmaking.

Helen Quinn

HELEN QUINN, 1995. THE 38" BY 38" WALL-HANGING WAS HAND-QUILTED BY HELEN IN 1992. THE PATTERN IS A TRADITIONAL ONE, "WHEEL OF FORTUNE."

Janice Dayton

JANICE DAYTON, 1995. THE 72" BY 54" BED QUILT, "OLD NINE-PATCH," WAS HAND-QUILTED BY JANICE IN 1993. IT IS A "NEW QUILT MADE TO LOOK LIKE AN OLD QUILT," JANICE WROTE.

Five women are honored this day for their talents and contribution to the region's quilted art: Janice Dayton of Woodstock, Ulster County; Vija Clark of Kingston, Ulster County; Dessa Hague of Tannersville, Greene County; Helen Quinn of Accord, Ulster County; and Marie Kremer of Claryville, Sullivan County.

Their origins provide an interesting commentary on the changing face of the Catskills: none of them was born here. Dessa Hague and Marie Kremer were "neighbors," growing up in Hamilton, New York, and Brooklyn, respectively, while Helen Quinn is from Seattle, Janice Dayton from Michigan, and Vija Clark from Latvia. But they all found an enduring home in the Catskills and a sort of symbiosis ensued; their art flowered and the region's culture was enriched as the spirit of the Catskills entered and took root in their souls. In true melting pot fashion, a fine alloy is the result.

Dessa Hague learned quiltmaking from her grandmother and mother back in the 1920s and 1930s in western New York, and produced over 115 quilts during her seventy-seven years, the last fifty-six of which were spent in the Catskills. Marie Kremer, Janice Dayton, Helen Quinn and Vija Clark all began to pursue the art after the quiltmaking renaissance began in the 1970s. They had the resources of organizations such as the Calico Geese, Wiltwyck and the South Mountain Piecemakers to draw upon (and contribute towards), as well as experienced teachers such as Ruth Culver, and the living example of the Claryville Ladies Aid.

Dessa Hague's sponsor was hard-pressed to supply sufficient examples of her work for the Hall of Fame selection committee because Dessa had given away so many of her quilts to various charities or family members. The rest had been sold. At the Patchworkers quilt show in August, 1993, one of Dessa's quilts sold for $800, a very handsome price for a traditional American quilt in the post-"Chinese quilt" days.

The majority of the quilts made by Vija Clark, Janice Dayton, Helen Quinn and Marie Kremer are not for sale, however. They are destined, for the most part, for family members, the walls and beds of their own homes, or to benefit charitable causes like church support, battered women's shelters, AIDS patients, or homes for the elderly.

Dessa Hague, the first inductee ever to be honored posthumously, was from the "old school," favoring large floor quilt frames. Her hus-

Dessa Hague

DESSA HAGUE, AIRING ONE OF HER MANY HAND-QUILTED BED QUILTS. PHOTOGRAPH FROM THE COLLECTION OF THE CATSKILL MOUNTAIN QUILTERS HALL OF FAME.

band and friends at the induction ceremony reminisced about how Dessa would bang on the overhead pipes of her basement workroom to get her husband's attention so he would know it was time to come downstairs and help her roll the quilt on the frame.

Helen Quinn, who learned to quilt around 1980, prefers lap quilting, even for king-sized quilts such as her white-on-white "Fan" quilt which was featured in a 1993 issue of *House and Gardens*. Marie Kremer has a special penchant (and eye for color) for "stained glass" quilts. Janice Dayton is known for her "Flower Basket" quilts and wall-hangings. And Vija Clark likes to experiment with new versions of old standards, such as crazy quilts and "Nine-Block," adding, as she says, "maybe ... just a little new original twist."

They are different from each other, these quiltmakers, as different as the works they create. Part of the pleasure in viewing quilts at a show is seeing the marvelous variety of color and design that the human imagination can create from simple materials. Give a thousand quiltmakers the same few pieces of patterned or plain cloth and the result will be a thousand different unique works of art. But the spirit will remain the same:

> *I start anyplace. I might use a pattern, or a scrap of fabric, or color, or might have a special purpose. It is like a seed that keeps on growing till it becomes a full-grown project. Many times I sit at my kitchen table having cup after cup of coffee, stare out the window and lovingly handle this "seed." Then suddenly it starts growing so fast I just try to keep up with it by shopping for fabric, going through all the boxes I have home, washing, ironing, cutting, changing something, cutting again, going for more fabric in different colors. I think about it while driving to work. If a friend calls, I tell them I am on high (then explain it is high on quilting). Some nights it is hard to fall asleep when designs, like sugarplums, dance in my head ... I buy [fabrics] in shops, yard sales, get it from friends, or beg for it. I could not wait for my youngest son to outgrow a very nice shirt so I could cut it up ... Why do I quilt? I have to! Just like I have to get up in the morning and go to rest at night ... It is giving a part of our heart to life that is endless.* [Vija Clark, 1993, inducted into the Catskill Mountain Quilters Hall of Fame 1994]

Vija Clark

VIJA CLARK, 1995. THE 96" BY 112" BED QUILT, "FOOL'S PUZZLE," WAS VIJA'S
FIRST PIECED QUILT, HAND-PIECED AND HAND-QUILTED IN 1978.

Notes for Chapter 2

1. Dolores A. Hinson, *Quilting Manual* (New York: Dover Publications, Inc., 1980), 90.

2. Lenice Ingram Bacon, *American Patchwork Quilts* (New York: Bonanza Books, 1980), 161.

3. Gene Sloan, "Resurgence in quilting celebrates a stitch in time," *USA Today* (October 11, 1993): 4D.

4. Jacqueline M. Atkins and Phyllis A. Fepper, *New York Beauties, Quilts from the Empire State* (New York: Dutton Studio Books, 1992), 4.

5. Ibid., 117.

6. Carter Houck, "From the Mountains ... to the City ... to the Towns that Lie Between ... " *Lady's Circle Patchwork Quilts* (January, 1985).

7. *New York Beauties,* 123.

8. Ibid., 80.

9. Doris West Brooks, "Mountain Top Historical Society receives Gift of Two Quilts," *The Hemlock* (Summer, 1994).

10. *New York Beauties,* 27.

11. Ibid., 114.

12. Joyce Ice and Linda Norris, eds., *Quilted Together: Women, Quilts, and Communities* (Delhi, NY: Delaware County Historical Association, 1989), 7, 31.

13. Ibid., 12.

14. In the Bronck House Museum collection.

15. *New York Beauties,* 49.

16. Susan Jenkins and Linda Seward, *The American Quilt Story: The How To and Heritage of a Craft Tradition* (Emmaus, PA: Rodale Press, 1991), 98.

17. *New York Beauties,* 35.

18. *USA Today* (October 11, 1993), 4D.

19. *Quilter's Newsletter Magazine,* Vol. 9, #8 (October 1993).

Sources Consulted

The primary sources for this book were interviews with quiltmakers who had been inducted into the Catskill Mountain Quilters Hall of Fame, taped by the author in 1993 and 1994. Supporting those interviews were questionnaires completed by those quiltmakers, and by many others who were not (or not yet) inductees, together with miscellaneous documents from the Catskill Mountain Quilters Hall of Fame and various member guilds, including the "Secretary's Report" of the Claryville Ladies Aid Society, and a diary kept by the Ladies Sewing Circle of Mitchell Hollow Road.

Published works consulted are as follows:

Atkins, Jacqueline M., and Phyllis A. Fepper. *New York Beauties, Quilts from the Empire State*. New York: Dutton Studio Books, 1992.

Bacon, Lenice Ingram. *American Patchwork Quilts*. New York: Bonanza Books, 1980.

Benincasa, Janis. *Catskill Mountain Quilters Hall of Fame*. Arkville, NY: The Erpf Catskill Cultural Center, 1986.

Bishop, Robert and Elizabeth Safunda. *A Gallery of Amish Quilts, Design Diversity from a Plain People*. New York: E. P. Dutton & Co., Inc., 1976.

Brackman, Barbara. *Clues in the Calico, A Guide to Identifying and Dating Antique Quilts*. McLean, VA: EPM Publications, Inc., 1989.

Brooks, Doris. "Mountain Top Historical Society receives Gift of two Quilts." *The Hemlock* (Summer, 1994).

———. "'The Patchworkers Guild' and a Short Story of Quilt Making." *Kaatskill Life*, Vol. 3, #3 (Fall, 1988).

Buckley, Bruce. *Folk Arts: Living Tradition; Folk Arts in Schoharie County*. Cobleskill, NY: Schoharie County Arts Council, 1989.

Bullard, Lacy Folmar, and Betty Jo Shiell. *Chintz Quilts: Unfading Glory*. Tallahassee, FL: Serendipity Publishers, 1983.

Christensen, Erwin O. *American Crafts and Folk Arts*. Washington, DC: Robert B. Bruce, Inc., 1964.

Colby, Averil. *Quilting*. New York: Charles Scribner's Sons, 1979.

Dee, Anne Paterson. *Quilter's Sourcebook*. Lombard, IL: Wallace-Homestead Book Company, 1987.

Duke, Dennis, and Deborah Harding, eds. *America's Glorious Quilts.* New York: Park Lane, 1989.

Firelands Association for the Visual Arts. *Quilts and Carousels: Folk Art in the Firelands.* Oberlin, Ohio: Press of the Times, 1983.

Hinson, Dolores A. *Quilting Manual.* New York: Dover Publications, Inc., 1980

Horne, Field. *Mountaintop and Valley, Greene County Folk Arts Today.* Hensonville, NY: Black Dome Press, 1991.

–––. *Traditional Folk Art of Montgomery County, New York.* Fort Johnson, NY: Montgomery County Historical Society, 1989.

Houck, Carter. "From the Mountains ... to the City ... to the Towns that Lie Between ... ". *Lady's Circle Patchwork Quilts* (January, 1985).

Houck, Carter, and Myron Miller. *American Quilts and How to Make Them.* New York: Charles Scribner's Sons, 1975.

Ice, Joyce, and Linda Norris, eds. *Quilted Together: Women, Quilts, and Communities.* Delhi, NY: Delaware County Historical Association, 1989.

Jenkins, Susan, and Linda Seward. *The American Quilt Story: The How To and Heritage of a Craft Tradition.* Emmaus, PA: Rodale Press, 1991.

Kiracofe, Roderick, ed. *The Quilt Digest.* San Francisco: Kiracofe & Kile, 1983.

–––, ed. *The Quilt Digest.* San Francisco: Kiracofe & Kile, 1984.

Lewis, Alfred Allan. *The Mountain Artisans Quilting Book.* New York: MacMillan Publishing Co., Inc., 1973.

Lipsett, Linda Otto. *Remember Me, Women & Their Friendship Quilts.* San Francisco: The Quilt Digest Press, 1985.

Mosey, Caron L. *America's Pictorial Quilts.* Paducah, KY: American Quilter's Society, 1985.

Packer, Barbara, ed. *The State of the Art Quilt: Contemporary Quilts for the Collector.* Friends of Nassau County Recreation, 1985.

Pellman, Rachel T., and Joanne Ranck. *Quilts Among the Plain People.* Lancaster, PA: Good Books, 1981.

Quilter's Newsletter Magazine, Vol. 25, #8 (October, 1993).

Robinson, Charlotte. *The Artist & the Quilt.* New York: Alfred A. Knopf, Inc., 1983.

Ruskin, Cindy. *The Quilt, Stories from the NAMES Project.* New York:

Pocket Books, 1988.

Safford, Carleton L., and Robert Bishop. *America's Quilts and Coverlets.* New York: E. P. Dutton, 1980.

Sloan, Gene. "Resurgence in quilting celebrates a stitch in time." *USA Today* (October 11, 1993): 4D.

Webster, Marie D. *Quilts: Their Story and How to Make Them.* Santa Barbara, CA: Practical Patchwork, 1990.

ALSO AVAILABLE FROM BLACK DOME PRESS ....

For ordering information: Black Dome Press, RR 1, Box 422,
Hensonville, NY, 12439. Tel: 518-734-6357

DIAMOND STREET The Story of the Little Town with the Big Red Light District,
by Bruce Edward Hall
Hudson, NY, pop. 8000, a Norman Rockwell painting in motion, with
one big difference–for almost two centuries this little city by the Hudson
River held an international reputation as a center for corruption and vice.
222 pp, 43 illustrations, Paper, $13.95

THE CATSKILL MOUNTAIN HOUSE America's Grandest Hotel, by Roland
Van Zandt
Captures the birth, glory and fiery death of America's premier mountain
resort. Best known for inspiring the Hudson River School of painting, for 140
years the Catskill Mountain House stood on a rock shelf above the hudson
valley and facing the River.
416 pp, 94 illustrations, 9 maps, Paper: $19.95, Cloth: $31.95

A VISIBLE HERITAGE Columbia County, New York: A History in Art &
Architecture, by Ruth Piwonka and Roderic H. Blackburn
157 photographs grace this pioneer work which traces 300 years of artists'
and architects' impressions and renderings of one of the earliest regions of
European settlement.
160 pp, 157 illustrations, Paper: $24.95, Cloth: $34.95

PRINTER'S DEVIL TO PUBLISHER Adolph S. Ochs of The New York Times, by
Doris Faber, Introduction by Arthur Ochs Sulzberger Published as part of
the *Times*'s centennial celebration, and written by a former *Times* reporter,
this is the dramatic and little-known story of how a struggling young man
from Tennessee bought the nearly bankrupt *New York Times* in 1896 and
transformed it into the best and most powerful newspaper in the world.
192 pp, Paper, $12.95

PORTRAITS OF PRIDE The Mountaintop Remembers, by Richard Winter
As family farms fade away, taking with them a way of life and a lifelong sense
of values instilled in earliest childhood, the last remaining old-timers take a
look at the present day and compare it with the world they knew.
208 pp, 61 photographs, Paper, $19.95

THE GREENE COUNTY CATSKILLS *A History,* by Field Horne, Introduction by Mario Cuomo

Four hundred years of Hudson Valley history! *Historian Field Horne...is a font of knowledge and lively chronicler of folklore. The enchanting full-color cover—with Rip asleep on an old postcard of famous Catskill sites—is worth the price of the book.—* Albany Times Union

236 pp, 121 illustrations, Paper: $25.95, Cloth: $35.95

THE HUCKLEBERRY PICKERS *A Raucous History of the Shawangunk Mountains,* by Marc B. Fried

The hard-working days and rowdy nights of the squatters' camps, summer home to the berry-pickers—an isolated, clannish, proud and independent community of free spirits and families struggling to survive—generations of whom converged on the winding trails and rocky overlooks of the Minnewaska and Ellenville parklands to harvest the "blue gold" of the Shawangunks.

164 pp, maps & illustrations, Paper, $14.95

KAATERSKILL *From the Catskill Mountain House to the Hudson River School,* by The Mountain Top Historical Society

The home and haunt of America's Romantic-era landscape painters, the grand hotels, and the golden age of railroads. *For those interested in the Catskills, or in mountains, or in history, or in fascinating places.—* Adirondack Mountain Club

120 pp, 33 illustrations, Paper, $13.95

THE MILL *on the Roeliff Jansen Kill,* by the Roeliff Jansen Historical Society

Built in 1743 by the Livingstons, the Mill has survived more than 250 years of political and economic change. *The story of New York State's oldest operating mill is also the story of the Hudson Valley.* The Northern Centinel

144 pp, 36 photographs, 2 maps, Paper, $15.00

THE OLD EAGLE-NESTER *The Lost Legends of the Catskills,* by Doris West Brooks

This is wonderful stuff, some of it funny, some of it frightening, all of it entertaining. Dutchess Magazine

128 pp, original illustrations, Paper, $13.95

EYE Pioneering Photographers in Rural Upstate, by
Diane Galusha
Turn-of-the-century rural New York as seen through the eyes of three Catskill
Mountain farmers' daughters. *The rediscovery of a lost chapter in the history of
photography.* Daily Gazette

5

Story of What Happened to the

ees blanketed the Catskill
not to be found today, felled
complex international oper-
antebellum America.

st, *Windham, New York,* by

d to a lonely, isolated, unin-
l in the winter of 1795, and

on, by Philip H. Dubois
ntury childhood growing up

rts Today, by Field Horne
ed in this Heritage Award-

Coxsackie, Earlton & Climax

way to the West, to bucol-